W9-DDP-061

REGENTS RESTORATION DRAMA SERIES

General Editor: John Loftis

THE BEAUX' STRATAGEM

GEORGE FARQUHAR

The Beaux' Stratagem

Edited by

CHARLES N. FIFER

UNIVERSITY OF NEBRASKA PRESS • LINCOLN

Publishers on the Plains

UNP

Library of Congress Cataloging in Publication Data
Farquhar, George, 1677?–1707.
  The beaux' stratagem.

  (Regents restoration drama series)
  I. Fifer, Charles N., 1922–   II. Title.
PR3437 B4 1977   822'.4   77–89834
ISBN 0–8032–5384–2
ISBN 0–8032–0384–5

MANUFACTURED IN THE UNITED STATES OF AMERICA

Regents Restoration Drama Series

The Regents Restoration Drama Series provides soundly edited texts, in modern spelling, of the more significant plays of the late seventeenth and early eighteenth centuries. The word "Restoration" is here used ambiguously and must be explained. A strict definition of the word is unacceptable to everyone, for it would exclude, among many other plays, those of Congreve. If to the historian it refers to the period between 1660 and 1685 (or 1688), it has long been used by the student of drama in default of a more precise term to refer to plays belonging to the dramatic tradition established in the 1660s, weakening after 1700, and displaced in the 1730s. It is in this extended sense—imprecise though justified by academic custom—that the word is used in this series, which includes plays first produced between 1660 and 1737. Although these limiting dates are determined by political events, the return of Charles II (and the removal of prohibitions against operation of theaters) and the passage of Walpole's Stage Licensing Act, they enclose a period of dramatic history having a coherence of its own in the establishment, development, and disintegration of a tradition.

The editors have planned the series with attention to the projected dimensions of the completed whole, a representative collection of Restoration drama providing a record of artistic achievement and providing also a record of the deepest concerns of three generations of Englishmen. And thus it contains deservedly famous plays—*The Country Wife, The Man of Mode,* and *The Way of the World*—and also significant but little known plays, *The Virtuoso,* for example, and *City Politiques,* the former a satirical review of scientific investigation in the early years of the Royal Society, the latter an equally satirical review of politics at the time of the Popish Plot. If the volumes of famous plays finally achieve

v

the larger circulation, the other volumes may have the greater utility, in making available texts otherwise difficult of access with the editorial apparatus needed to make them intelligible. The editors have had the instructive example of the parallel and senior project, the Regents Renaissance Drama Series; they have in fact used the editorial policies developed for the earlier plays as their own, modifying them as appropriate for the later period and as the experience of successive editions suggested. The introductions to the separate Restoration plays differ considerably in their nature. Although a uniform body of relevant information is presented in each of them, no attempt has been made to impose a pattern of interpretation. Emphasis in the introductions has necessarily varied with the nature of the plays and inevitably—we think desirably—with the special interests and aptitudes of the different editors.

Each text in the series is based on a fresh collation of the seventeenth- and eighteenth-century editions that might be presumed to have authority. The textual notes, which appear above the rule at the bottom of each page, record all substantive departures from the edition used as the copy-text. Variant substantive readings among contemporary editions are listed there as well. Editions later than the eighteenth century are referred to in the textual notes only when an emendation originating in some one of them is received into the text. Variants of accidentals (spelling, punctuation, capitalization) are not recorded in the notes except in instances in which they have, or may have, substantive relevance. Contracted forms of characters' names are silently expanded in speech prefixes and stage directions and, in the case of speech prefixes, are regularized. Additions to the stage directions of the copy-text are enclosed in brackets.

Spelling has been modernized along consciously conservative lines, but within the limits of a modernized text the linguistic quality of the original has been carefully preserved. Contracted preterites have regularly been expanded. Punctuation has been brought into accord with modern practices. The objective has been to achieve a balance between the pointing of the old editions and a system of punctuation which, without overloading the text with exclamation marks, semicolons, and dashes, will make the often loosely flowing verse and prose of the original syntactically intelligible to the modern reader. Dashes are regularly used only to indicate interrupted speeches, or shifts of address within a single speech.

Explanatory notes, chiefly concerned with glossing obsolete words and phrases, are printed below the textual notes at the bottom of each page. References to stage directions in the notes follow the admirable system of the Revels editions, whereby stage directions are keyed, decimally, to the line of the text before or after which they occur. Thus, a note on 0.2 has reference to the second line of the stage direction at the beginning of the scene in question. A note on 115.1 has reference to the first line of the stage direction following line 115 of the text of the relevant scene. Speech prefixes, and any stage directions attached to them, are keyed to the first line of accompanying dialogue.

JOHN LOFTIS

Stanford University

Contents

Regents Restoration Drama Series   v

List of Abbreviations   xi

Introduction   xiii

THE BEAUX' STRATAGEM   1

Appendix A: Variant Passages from *The Works*, Sixth Edition   133

Appendix B: Chronology   135

List of Abbreviations

Archer	William Archer. *George Farquhar*. London, 1906.
C	*The Comedies of Mr. George Farquhar*. London, 1708.
C5	*The Comedies of Mr. George Farquhar*. 5th ed. London, 1721.
D1	Duodecimo, 10th ed., Dublin, 1724.
D2	Duodecimo, 7th ed., London, 1730.
Gosse	Edmund Gosse, ed. *Restoration Plays*. Everyman Edition. London, 1912.
Inchbald	Elizabeth Inchbald, ed. *The British Theatre*, vol. 8. London, 1808.
Larson	Martin A. Larson. "The Influence of Milton's Divorce Tracts on Farquhar's *Beaux' Stratagem*," *PMLA* 39 (1924): 174–78.
O	Octavo, London, 1710.
OED	*Oxford English Dictionary*
om.	omitted
Q1	First quarto, 1707.
Q2	Second quarto ("The Second Edition"), 1707.
S.D.	stage direction
S.P.	speech prefix
Stonehill	*The Complete Works of George Farquhar*. Ed. Charles Stonehill. 2 vols. New York, 1930.
W2	*The Works of the Late Ingenious Mr. George Farquhar*. 2nd ed. London, 1711.
W6	*The Works of the Late Ingenious Mr. George Farquhar*. 6th ed. London, 1728.

Introduction

On 27 January 1707, Bernard Lintot purchased the manuscript of *The Beaux' Stratagem* from George Farquhar for £30, almost twice as much as he had paid for *The Recruiting Officer* the preceding winter.[1] Exactly two months later, on 27 March,[2] he published the first edition (Q1) of the play. According to Allardyce Nicoll[3] and both the first and second editions of the *Cambridge Bibliography of English Literature*, there were nine editions published in 1707, the first undated. These nine "editions" are clearly variant states of the same edition, all undated on their title pages. Even though there are anomalies in some of these states (in one of the Bodleian copies [Mal.138(7)] the Epilogue and Dramatis Personae precede the Advertisement and Prologue), the type of all the copies I have examined is the same.[4] The second edition, undated, but identified on the title page as "The Second Edition," was published, it is generally assumed, in the same year as the first. It is virtually a page-by-page reprint of the first edition with a number of changes and corrections, although there is an additional line on page 45 that carries over to page 46; page 47 contains one line less than the original, so that the pagination of the first edition resumes on page 48.

Because of his death so soon after the publication of the first edition, it seems doubtful that Farquhar had anything to do with the changes made in the second. Furthermore, the nature of most of the changes suggests a reviser alien to the spirit of the play. Aside from frequent and not always logical changes of punctua-

[1]"Bernard and Henry Lintot," *Literary Anecdotes of the Eighteenth Century*, ed. John Nichols (London, 1814), 8: 296.

[2]*The Daily Courant*, 27 March 1707.

[3]*A History of English Drama, 1660–1900* (Cambridge, 1952), 2: 322.

[4]The experience of A. N. Jeffares and Shirley Strum Kenny, who have collated a number of other copies (in addition to some I have checked), confirms mine. See their exchange of letters in *Times Literary Supplement*, 23 July and 21 Sept. 1971, pp. 861, 1119; and Jeffares's edition of *The Beaux' Stratagem* (Edinburgh, 1972), pp. 17–18.

tion and the correction of obvious typographical errors (as well as creation of others), there are essentially two kinds of changes found in the second edition, neither of which Farquhar is likely to have made—or even approved of. First of all, there is a consistent and somewhat schoolmarmish effort to standardize or modernize spelling and usage. *Shreeks* becomes *shrieks, perswading* becomes *persuading, do's* becomes *does;* a participle is substituted for a preterite form in "we came off with flying colors, *shew'd* no signs of want" (*shewing* in the second edition). More damaging to the spirit of the play, however, are the changes seemingly based on a desire to avoid informality or vulgarity. Contractions are consistently removed regardless of the speaker: *in't* becomes *in it* (Scrub), *with'em* becomes *with them* (Archer), *for't* becomes *for it* (Mrs. Sullen), *shannot* becomes *shall not* (Dorinda); or a more elegant contraction replaces an existing one: *keep'em* is substituted for *keep'um* (Mrs. Sullen) and *on'em* for *on'um* (Gibbet). One, but not all, of Scrub's *a-Sunday*'s becomes *on Sunday*. Most damaging, however, is the rather inconsistent removal of dialect. Archer, when speaking in brogue to Foigard, says *together* rather than *togeder*. Foigard says *that* rather than *dat*. Count Bellair refers to a *hundred* pound rather than to a *hundre* pound.

Because of the unlikelihood of Farquhar's participation in any but the first edition, I have used as copy-text the Yale University Library copy of that edition (Q1) and collated it with copies in the British Museum Library, the Bodleian Library (two copies), Harvard University Library, the National Library of Scotland, the University of Michigan Library, and the Boston Public Library. There are no substantive variants among these copies. I have also collated it with the University of Michigan copy of the second edition (Q2). I have examined a number of other eighteenth-century editions, both single and collected, in an effort to find emendations that have anticipated mine. These editions include *The Comedies of Mr. George Farquhar* [1708],[5] apparently the first collection of his works; *The Beaux Stratagem,* London, 1710; *The Works of the Late Ingenious Mr. George Farquhar,* 2nd ed., 1711;[6]

---

[5] Until Shirley Strum Kenny established the correct date for this edition (*TLS*, 21 Sept. 1971, p. 1119), it had been variously dated as 1707, 1709, and 1710.

[6] No first edition has been discovered. Kenny (*TLS*) has pointed out that this edition is a reprint of two earlier publications: *The Comedies,* 1708, and

The Beaux Stratagem, Edinburgh, 1715; *The Works,* 3rd ed., 1714; *The Works,* 6th ed., 1728,[7] apparently the first edition to indicate cuts frequently made in performance and to print in full the songs in Acts I and III; and *The Dramatick Works of Mr. George Farquhar,* 7th ed., 1736.[8] Most of the editions I have examined seem to have been based on Q1, or on early editions other than Q2; for although many of the corrections and modernizations found in Q2 appear, few of its arbitrary changes and scarcely any of its peculiar errors turn up. I cite modern editions only in instances in which they include emendations I have not found in eighteenth-century editions. I include in the textual notes a limited number of variants from editions lacking any authorial intervention partly to indicate the sort of deterioration that took place in later texts, and partly—and more importantly—to suggest the nature of the deliberate changes made by managers for their productions.

In normalizing the punctuation I have tried to retain the movement of Farquhar's brisk and often racy prose while, at the same time, suggesting more clearly than the original punctuation does the specific relationships existing among the various ele-

---

1702, a miscellany of Farquhar's letters, poems, and his "Discourse Upon Comedy."

[7]The general title page of the second volume, in which *The Beaux' Stratagem* appears, reads *"The Comedies of Mr. George Farquhar . . .* The Fifth Edition . . . 1728." The individual title page of the play is also dated 1728. I have not been able to find a 1728 edition of *The Comedies* that prints the songs, if one exists. The only copy of the 5th edition of *The Comedies* I have been able to inspect (Bodleian Vet. A4. 427, 428) is dated 1721, the date coming from a second general title page in the first volume (reading *"The Works . . .* The Fifth Edition . . . 1721"). The second volume, containing *The Beaux' Stratagem* and also dated 1721, is called "The Fourth Edition." This discrepancy of titles and/or editions (and even dates) is common to the collected editions of Farquhar's works. In a copy of the 4th edition of *The Works,* dated 1718, in the British Museum, all the plays in the first volume are dated 1735, those in the second, including *The Beaux' Stratagem,* 1736. Another copy, at Brown University, consists of a 4th edition first volume dated 1718, and an 8th edition second volume dated 1742. These are admittedly extreme examples; more usual is a copy of the 5th edition of *The Works,* 1721, at the Newberry Library, the second volume of which has a title page reading, *"The Comedies . . .* The Fourth Edition . . . 1721."

[8]There are at least three states of this edition, one containing the 7th (1730) edition of *The Beaux' Stratagem,* another the 8th (1733), and a third, dated 1736. The three states of the play vary in no substantive way.

ments of his often long and convoluted sentences. This process results sometimes in lightening or reducing the force of the original punctuation, or occasionally in increasing the number of marks of punctuation, or, probably most often, in finding modern equivalents for what seems to be, but in fact is not, a rather slapdash system of pointing. Boniface's description of Lady Bountiful in Act I (ll. 67–77) can serve as an example of my procedure. First, as in Q1:

> My Lady Bountiful is one of the best of women: Her last husband Sir Charles Bountiful left her worth a thousand pound a year; and I believe she lays out one half on't in charitable uses for the good of her neighbors; she cures rheumatisms, ruptures, and broken shins in men, green sickness, obstructions, and fits of the mother in women;—the king's-evil, chin-cough, and chilblains in children; in short, she has cured more people in and about Lichfield within ten years than the doctors have killed in twenty; and that's a bold word.

The passage, as repointed, reads thus:

> My Lady Bountiful is one of the best of women. Her last husband, Sir Charles Bountiful, left her worth a thousand pound a year, and I believe she lays out one half on't in charitable uses for the good of her neighbors. She cures rheumatisms, ruptures, and broken shins in men; green sickness, obstructions, and fits of the mother in women; the king's evil, chin-cough, and chilblains in children. In short, she has cured more people in and about Lichfield within ten years than the doctors have killled in twenty, and that's a bold word.

The Beaux' Stratagem was first performed at the Queen's Theatre in the Haymarket, on 8 March 1707, and was an immediate success. It was played twelve more times that season. For the next one hundred years, it was presented at theaters in and around London, and at Bath and Dublin, sometimes as often as fifteen or twenty times a season. In the last quarter of the eighteenth century, the number of performances occasionally dwindled to one or two each season, but at almost no time during this long period does it seem to have been absent from the stage.[9] Genest records two performances at Drury Lane in the centenary season of 1806–1807, and the play continued to be produced with some regularity for the next seventeen years. Interest in it seems to have faded after the 1822–23 season, until on 31 December 1828, Covent Garden revived it with Charles Kemble in the role of Archer.[10] The company staged the play eleven more times that season, a number that suggests that it pleased audiences. Occasional performances were presented throughout the nineteenth and twentieth centuries,[11] the latest in 1970 by the National Theatre in London.

The Beaux' Stratagem was apparently a favorite with actors, and the fact that many of the most popular actors performed in it undoubtedly contributed to its lasting popularity. Farquhar's friend Robert Wilks, the original Archer, played the role frequently until shortly before his death in 1732. For over thirty years after 1721, Lacey Ryan portrayed Archer with considerable success. In the years between Wilks's death and the advent of probably the most popular Archer of all time, David Garrick, William Mills took the role at Drury Lane. Garrick, between 22 December 1742, the date of his first appearance as Archer, and June 1776, when he retired from the stage, appeared as Archer frequently almost every season; it was one of his most successful roles. His life-long friend, Samuel Johnson, however, believed that he did not play the part well. "The gentleman should break out through the footman, which is not the case as he does it."[12] Garrick occasionally played Scrub, usually when his protegé, William O'Brien, appeared as Archer. Other Archers in these and later years were William Smith and Thomas Lewis, the latter of

---

[9] Neither John Genest, *Some Account of the English Stage, from the Restoration in 1660 to 1830* (Bath, 1832), vol. 8, nor Charles Beecher Hogan, *The London Stage 1660–1800, Part V: 1776–1800* (Carbondale, Ill., 1968), Vol. 3, records a performance in the 1795–96 season. It seems likely, however, that somewhere in Great Britain that season *The Beaux' Stratagem* was performed.

[10] Genest, 9: 476.

[11] According to Charles Stonehill, *The Complete Works of George Farquhar* (New York, 1930), 2: 121, "there was scarcely any period since its first production when it can be said to have been 'forgotten.'"

[12] *Boswell's Life of Johnson,* ed. G. B. Hill and L. F. Powell (Oxford, 1934–50), 3: 52.

whom performed the role into the nineteenth century both at Drury Lane and at Covent Garden. Charles Kemble also portrayed Archer during the first quarter of the nineteenth century.

The less interesting role of Aimwell seems to have been taken by a number of actors who, like Mills, later graduated to the role of Archer. Dennis Delane and John Palmer, both of whom were Aimwell to Garrick's Archer, also appeared as Archer. William Farren, who for a number of years had acted Aimwell at Covent Garden, appeared as Archer at Bath in November 1817. Much more popular with both actors and audiences was the role of Scrub, played by most of the leading comic actors of their time. It was performed successfully in the eighteenth century by, among others, Henry Norris, the first Scrub; William Penkethman; Theophilus Cibber, the son of the original Gibbet, Colley Cibber; John Hippisley; Charles Macklin and Richard Yates, both of whom played frequently with Garrick at Drury Lane; Edward Shuter, who was later such a success as Croaker in Goldsmith's *The Good Natured Man,* and who had acted Gibbet a number of times; and Henry Woodward.

Even the less important comic male roles have attracted a number of distinguished actors over the years. Richard Estcourt and James Quin were two of the earlier interpreters of Sullen; Cibber, Macklin, and Yates, and notably John Barrington, an Irishman,[13] of Foigard; and Woodward and Shuter, like the elder Cibber, of Gibbet.

Of the female roles, Mrs. Sullen has been the most popular with actresses ever since Anne Oldfield first took the part (and she continued to play it until she died in 1730). Both Hannah Pritchard, who had previously acted Dorinda, and Peg Woffington frequently appeared in the role opposite Garrick's Archer at Drury Lane; and Garrick continued to be lucky in his female stage partners when he was joined later by Frances Abington. "No actress," Genest reports, "who has succeeded Mrs. Abington in . . Mrs. Sullen . . . has been equal to her." She was undoubtedly more than equaled by her successors in the role of Scrub, which, in an ill-advised moment, she chose for her benefit on 10 Feb-

---

[13]P. H. Highfill, Jr., K. A. Burnim, E. A. Langhans, *A Biographical Dictionary of Actors, Actresses . . . in London, 1660–1800* (Carbondale and Edwardsville, Ill., 1973), 1: 310.

ruary 1786. "For this aberration she was roundly abused in the papers."[14] Her less fortunate successors in the role of Mrs. Sullen included, in the eighteenth century, Mrs. Ann Spranger Barry, Elizabeth Farren, and Elizabeth Pope. In the first decades of the nineteenth century, Mrs. Charles Kemble was probably the best-known interpreter of the part; in the twentieth century, both Dame Edith Evans (1947) and Maggie Smith (1970) have played it. The other popular female role, Cherry, has been undertaken by a number of well-known actresses, among them Lavinia Fenton (known as "Polly" because of her great success in *The Beggar's Opera*), Mrs. Woffington, Jane Pope, Mrs. Abington, and Mrs. Charles Kemble.

No well-known actor is traditionally associated with the role of Count Bellair; it seems that very early in the long and successful career of *The Beaux' Stratagem* the Count did not appear in most performances and was merely referred to by other characters. There may have been several reasons for his removal: perhaps the part proved unsuccessful with its first audience either for dramatic or for moralistic reasons (Mrs. Sullen's deliberate leading-on of the Count in order to make her husband jealous could have diminished her attractiveness to the audience and diminished as well the very real pathos evoked by her situation); perhaps the Count was considered by Farquhar and the managers of the Haymarket the character most easily dispensed with when it was found necessary to shorten the time of performance; or perhaps anti-French feeling made his part unpopular. According to a note to Act III, scene iii (ll. 310.1 ff. in this edition), which first appears in the sixth edition of the *Works* (1728): "This scene printed in *italic*, with the entire part of the *Count*, was cut out by the Author, after the first Night's Representation; and where he shou'd enter in the last Scene of the fifth Act, it is added to the Part of *Foigard*."

There is considerable evidence, both in eighteenth-century playbills and in numerous editions of the play, that the part was eliminated from most performances. Neither Genest nor *The London Stage* prints a cast list in which the Count appears, aside from the one for the first performance (and that one is taken, not from a playbill, but from the first edition). It is possible, but

---

[14]Genest, 7: 445; *A Biographical Dictionary*, 1: 18.

unlikely, that since the cast lists are almost always incomplete (at least for *The Beaux' Stratagem*) the omission of his name is not real evidence; it is significant, however, that he alone is always omitted. Gipsy, although frequently omitted in early cast lists, does appear with increasing regularity later on; Hounslow and Bagshot, who are of less importance in the play than Bellair, are included occasionally. Even the Countrywoman, a very minor character indeed, makes her appearance in a few of the printed lists.

Editions of the play, moreover, offer even more convincing evidence. Although the Count is listed in the Dramatis Personae in the sixth edition of *The Works,* and his scene with the Sullens (III.iii) is printed (in italics), his lines in Act V, scene iv, are given, with appropriate dialect changes, to Foigard. Similar treatment of the character appears in numerous other printings and editions, including the three versions of the play (1730, 1733, 1736) in the 7th edition of the *Dramatick Works* (1736), and in an edition of the play printed at Edinburgh in 1755 for G. Hamilton and J. Balfour, clearly related to the 1733 version. In later editions, such as those purporting to print the play as acted "at the Theatre-Royal in Drury Lane and Covent Garden,"[15] not only are the Count's lines in Act V, scene iv, given to Foigard, but the lines italicized, or otherwise set off, in Act III, scene iii, of the editions described above are totally eliminated. The role of the Count does not appear in the cast lists of either theater printed at the beginning of the play.

More than the role of the Count was eliminated in performance,[16] however, as one can clearly see in the numerous editions

[15]One published by J. Rivington, W. Johnston, S. Crowder and Co., B. Law, T. Lownds, T. Caslon, and G. Kearsley (London, 1763), the other by W. Johnston, T. Lowndes, T. Caslon, W. Nicoll, and S. Bladon (London, 1768).

[16]Willard Connely reports, citing Thomas Wilkes's Preface to *Farquhar's Works* (Dublin, 1775), that after the first performance of the play Richard Steele recommended that "Love's Catechism," the scene between Cherry and Archer in Act II, and also the scene between Boniface and Gibbet at the beginning of Act V, be eliminated. His recommendation was accepted, and the scenes were omitted for at least the next eight performances. "Otherwise," Connely adds, somewhat inaccurately, "the *Stratagem* as written played on in its conquering course" (*Young George Farquhar* [London, 1949], p. 299).

based on prompt copies and managers' books of the last quarter of the eighteenth and the earlier years of the nineteenth centuries.[17] One such, published in 1776, desires the reader "to observe, that the passages omitted in the Representation at the Theatres are here preserved, and marked with inverted commas; as from Line 3 to 26, in Page 9" (I.135–59).[18] The excisions apparently made at Covent Garden vary in extent from partial lines to whole episodes. The nature of a number of these excised passages is interesting in that more than simply a desire to shorten the play often seems to have motivated their removal.[19] The passage referred to in the notice to the reader is an exchange between Archer and Aimwell on poverty and the need to keep up appearances—a piece of vaguely satirical social criticism. A very few lines later, the two men's remarks on various kinds of epicureans (ll. 203–45), further social commentary, are eliminated. A similar

A performance scheduled for 26 August 1735, at the Haymarket, was described as "Newly Revis'd and Alter'd. N. B. The Reviser begs leave to observe, that tho' he thinks the Chief Characters in this Play, are drawn with a great deal of Life and Spirit; Yet that even in this very sprightly Play there are several very obvious Faults. That as the Character of the French Count, and that of the Irish Priest, are in no sort conducive to the Plot of the Play; they may therefore be look'd upon as superfluous: that the parting of Sullen and his Wife, is extremely unnatural; and that the Ending of the Play (with respect to Archer) is abrupt to a degree, &c. &c." The reviser, in order "to amend these Errors," has improved upon the play (Arthur H. Scouten, *The London Stage 1660–1800, Part Three: 1729–1747* [Carbondale, Ill., 1961], 1: 505).

[17]Consider, for instance, Mrs. Inchbald's edition of *The Beaux' Stratagem,* "printed under the authority of the managers from the prompt book," in her *The British Theatre* (London, 1808), Vol. 8; R. Cumberland's edition, "regulated from the prompt books," in his *The British Drama* (London, 1817), Vol. 4. With only minor variations, they omit the same passages as the 1776 edition.

[18]*The Beaux Stratagem . . . Marked with the Variations in the Manager's Book, at the Theatre-Royal in Covent Garden* (London: Printed for T. Lowndes, T. Caslon, W. Nicoll, and S. Bladon, 1776), verso t.p.

[19]Time is certainly the reason for eliminating certain lines of purple prose (IV.i.147–53, V.iv.34–36), the singing of "The Trifle" (III.iii.189–256), and, in later years, the comparison of the Duke of Marlborough and Alexander the Great (IV.i.288–293). Omitting certain bits of trivial stage business—Cherry's quick entrance and exit at the beginning of V.iii, or Lady Bountiful's rushing out to fetch three or four useless swords at the same point in the play—clearly shortens the running time of a performance, as does the elimination of the dance at the end of Act V.

passage on the stratagems resorted to by the poor man of fashion who is trying to disguise his poverty is removed at IV.ii.(11–28). Though none of these passages contributes directly to the development of the plot, they do add to our impression of the two beaux as clever men-about-town; more than almost any other speeches in the play, they remind the reader or audience of the sort of witty exchange indulged in by the rakes of earlier Restoration comedy. And it is possibly just for this reason that they were eliminated from performances taking place in the somewhat more bourgeois world of the eighteenth century.

Of greater interest, however, are the deletions involving Mrs. Sullen. Some of the minor ones seem designed to get rid of a kind of looseness of character or cynical rakishness that occasionally seems to affect her, as when she tells Dorinda, "And she's [woman in general] a fool that won't believe a man there [in his flattery] as much as she that believes him in anything else." (IV.i. 407–9), or when she admits a few lines later (ll. 443–44) that she is a "generous soul, easy and yielding to soft desires, a spacious heart where love and all his train might lodge." At least one double entendre is removed, again in a speech to Dorinda, where Mrs. Sullen mocks the younger woman's eagerness to bring about an interview with Aimwell and Archer. "Patience! You country ladies give no quarter if once you be entered"[20] (III.iii.274–275). Another deletion is the scene with the Countrywoman: one might argue that the joke Mrs. Sullen plays on the gullible woman and her subsequent conversation with Lady Bountiful (IV.i.9–68), in addition to being irrelevant to the plot and unnecessarily drawing out the action, reveal her to be unattractively coarse and unfeeling. And if the part of Count Bellair had not been excised for the reasons already suggested, it might well have been removed for Mrs. Sullen's sake; as mentioned above, her relationship with the Count is not a credit to her character, and it is she, not the Count, who asserts that his motives are as frivolous as hers.

It seems clear, however, that most of the deletions are a deliberate attempt to diminish the importance and the seriousness of the marriage-divorce theme, for not only is the scene between

[20]The words "easy . . . lodge" in the previous quotation, and "if once you be entered" in the present quotation, are contained within inverted commas in the 1776 edition. Oddly enough, the highly moral Mrs. Inchbald (1808) retains the first of these phrases.

Mrs. Sullen, the Count, and Squire Sullen removed, but so are Mrs. Sullen's and Dorinda's immediately subsequent and significant comments about "the unaccountable disaffections of wedlock" and the inadequacy of the courts to deal with the problem (III.iii.415–38). In addition, the verses comparing the concord of nature and of marriage, spoken by Mrs. Sullen at the close of the act (ll. 439–51), do not appear, even within inverted commas, in the 1776 edition.[21] Closely related to the marriage-divorce theme, of course, is Mrs. Sullen's brief speech on the status of English women that opens Act IV, scene i, and immediately precedes her teasing of the Countrywoman; and this too was clearly omitted from many performances. These omissions, then, meant that in some performances everything between III.iii.309 and IV.i.69 was skipped over,[22] resulting not only in a shorter play, but in one with a considerably less solid base in serious moral or social ideas.

There is no evidence that Farquhar himself was responsible for any of the cuts or minor changes made to the play other than, perhaps, the elimination of Count Bellair and the subsequent dialogue change referred to above. Certainly by the time of the first performance he was too ill to undertake much in the way of revision; and the cuts made, involving as they do very little in the way of changed or additional dialogue, could have been made by almost anyone connected with the production of the play. Since it is doubtful that Farquhar was responsible even for the revisions of *The Recruiting Officer* the previous year, when his health was better,[23] any such activity at this time seems even more unlikely.

[21]The 1763 and 1768 editions likewise do not print the verses. The 1755 edition, however, by omitting the inverted commas around the verses, suggests that at least in some performances Mrs. Sullen did recite them at the end of the act, even when the lines preceding them were omitted. A further deletion that is called for in Inchbald, but not in most other editions, is the passage in which the Sullens, during their agreement to disagree (V.iv), explain why they married—he for an heir, she for support of her feminine weakness and for pleasure in "agreeable society" (ll. 221–31). Unlike the brief passage from this exchange more often omitted in performance—the "vulture," "goblin," "porcupine," "wormwood" passage (ll. 241–45)—these lines at least touch on relatively serious concerns of marriage.

[22]As in the 1763, 1768, and 1776 editions, and also Inchbald and Cumberland.

[23]*The Recruiting Officer,* ed. Michael Shugrue (Lincoln, Nebr., 1965), p. xii.

Regardless, however, of who made the changes, the fact that a good many of them seem to have been made for moral reasons suggests that the aftershock of Jeremy Collier's attack of 1698, *A Short View of the Immorality and Profaneness of the English Stage,* continued beyond the years of the most intensive controversy raised by his pamphlet.

Collier, of course, did not initiate moral disapproval of the theater; he simply expressed a strongly growing tendency in society as a whole. Charles Harold Gray points out that nearly all the "dramatic criticism of the writers in the periodicals up to the end of the first thirty years of the eighteenth century . . . deals with the question of the morality of the drama in some way or other."[24] It was certainly the moral ambiguities of the play that troubled Mrs. Oldfield, the first Mrs. Sullen; Farquhar was told that "Mrs. Oldfield thought he had dealt too freely with the character of Mrs. Sullen in giving her to Archer, without such a proper divorce, as might be a security to her honour."[25] And the divorce, or lack of it, continued to be one of the elements troubling the play's critics and editors for decades after. An anonymous critic writing in the *London Chronicle* in 1757 and 1758 was shocked by the ending of the play and called the separation of the Sullens "unnatural."[26] Mrs. Sullen, according to Elizabeth Inchbald in 1808, "though pitiable . . . is no other than a deliberate violator of her marriage vow." Aimwell and Archer "are but arrant impostors"; and "all the wise and witty persons of this comedy are knaves, and all the honest people fools." "It is an honour to the morality of the present age," she smugly asserts, "that this most entertaining comedy is but seldom performed."[27] More than half a century later, Adolphus William Ward, while generally praising the play, regrets that "some of the incidents indeed are dubious, including one at the close,—a separation by mutual consent, which throws a glaring light on the view taken by the author and his age of the sanctity of the marriage-tie."[28] Even William Archer, whose com-

---

[24]Gray, *Theatrical Criticism in London to 1795* (New York, 1931), p. 64.
[25]Genest, 2: 366.

[26]Gray, *Theatrical Criticism,* pp. 134–35.

[27]"Remarks" preceding *The Beaux' Stratagem* in *The British Theatre,* Vol. 8.

[28]*A History of English Dramatic Literature to the Death of Queen Anne* (London, 1875), 2: 595.

ments on Farquhar are both sensible and sensitive and who finds a moral basis in the play, feels constrained to confess that the "ethical standards of . . . *The Beaux' Stratagem* cannot, certainly, be called high."[29] But Archer's assumption of the moral stance is brief and without great conviction, and most critics who have followed him have felt no need to apologize for Farquhar's morals,[30] but have been able to concentrate on the more interesting and important concerns of what Farquhar has to say and how he says it.

Few have denied that *The Beaux' Stratagem* is Farquhar's best play, or have disagreed about the reasons for its strong appeal. As early as 1840, Leigh Hunt presented the case for the play as vigorously and as accurately as anyone before or since:

> Its plot is new, simple, and interesting; the characters various, without confusing it; the dialogue sprightly and characteristic; the moral bold, healthy, admirable, and doubly needed in those times, when sottishness was a fashion. . . . The only fault in the termination, is what Mrs. Oldfield objected to,—that the law had provided no sanction for it; so that it became but a higher kind of sale by halter. But what a lesson did not this very want imply? The footsteps of the gravest ultimate reforms are often found in places where they are least looked for. But Nature speaks there, and there they come.[31]

But many, admitting its appeal, have had great trouble in defining exactly what the play is—the last of the traditional comedies of manners, the destroyer of that tradition, or the first comedy of a new tradition—and exactly what it attempts to say. A major cause

[29]*George Farquhar* (London and New York, 1906), p. 20.

[30]At least one modern commentator takes exception to Archer's effort to palliate Farquhar's immorality: "From the moral point of view, Aimwell's desire to marry a wealthy heiress by pretending to be a lord is worse than any action of Valentine or Mirabell [characters in Congreve's *Love for Love* and *The Way of the World*]; and the actions of Aimwell and Archer are not rendered more moral by the former's repentance or the latter's failure" (Kenneth Muir, *The Comedy of Manners* [London, 1970], p. 153).

[31]Biographical and Critical Notices to *The Dramatic Works of Wycherley, Congreve, Vanbrugh, and Farquhar*, new ed. (London, 1855), pp. lviii–lix.

of this uncertainty is that *The Beaux' Stratagem,* as generations of critics have pointed out, is a transitional work, sharing certain characteristics with the Restoration comedy of manners that preceded it and other characteristics with the chaster and more bland comedy that followed it. It seems to possess the casual attitude toward sex, the aristocratic amorality, the freedom of language and action associated with the plays of Etherege, Wycherley, and Congreve; but conventional virtue wins out at play's end. The bride is ultimately won not by wit or strategem, but by honesty— the result of true love. Farquhar seems to go out of his way to remind us both of his debt to his Restoration predecessors and of his differences from them. It has often been noted that Archer's attempted seduction of Mrs. Sullen resembles the seduction scene between Loveless and Berinthia in Vanbrugh's *The Relapse* (1696); the earlier seduction is, however, successful, mainly because the lady is more cooperative than Mrs. Sullen (her "cries" for help are barely audible). The discrepancies between the two scenes, which Farquhar's audiences would no doubt have perceived, would not only have struck them as amusing but would have also reminded them of the moral superiority of both Mrs. Sullen, who makes a serious effort to resist Archer, and the play in which she appeared. The Sullens' description in the last act of their incompatability also has its prototype in *The Relapse* in Berinthia's description of her and her late husband's inability to agree on anything but sleeping apart. In Vanbrugh's *The Provoked Wife,* Sir John Brute, like Mr. Sullen, comes home drunk and disturbs his sleeping wife. These resemblances to earlier drama, juxtaposed with the actions of Farquhar's play, further enforce the moral ironies implicit in the comparisons and contrasts.

Another of the principal means by which Farquhar combines these somewhat contradictory elements is the traditional device of the paired heroes. Archer possesses many of the qualities of the Restoration rake; he is a witty, amorous, and unprincipled hedonist. As Mrs. Sullen marvels, "The devil's in this fellow. He fights, loves, and banters, all in a breath." Many of his speeches stress his rakishness, his love of pleasure, his intelligent control of himself and the situations in which he is involved:

Give me a man that keeps his five senses keen and bright as his sword, that has 'em always drawn out in their just order and strength, with his reason as commander at the head of 'em, that detaches 'em by turns upon whatever party of pleasure agreeably offers, and commands 'em to retreat upon the least appearance of disadvantage or danger. For my part, I can stick to my bottle, while my wine, my company, and my reason holds good; I can be charmed with Sappho's singing without falling in love with her face; I love hunting, but would not, like Actaeon, be eaten up by my own dogs; I love a fine house, but let another keep it; and just so I love a fine woman.

(I.225–37)

Archer's most characteristic scenes are those in which he attempts to seduce, with enthusiastic élan, the women he meets, attached or unattached, and regardless of class (a social comedown from the likes of Congreve's Mirabell). And it seems clear that he would have consummated these seductions had he not been interrupted.

Archer, who must have appealed to the aristocratic element in Farquhar's audience, is balanced by Aimwell, the ultimately reformed rake, who must have been a more attractive character to the increasing numbers of merchants and others of similar status who attended the theater after 1688.[32] Starting out as a pale copy of Archer, Aimwell is ultimately converted by his love for Dorinda and her "matchless honesty," as she rather mistakenly calls his confession. The moment of his conversion could have come straight from the most sentimental of comedies:

Such goodness who could injure? I find myself unequal to the task of villain; she has gained my soul and made it honest like her own. I cannot, cannot hurt her. . . . Madam, behold your lover and your proselyte, and judge of my passion by my conversion. . . . I am no lord, but a poor needy man come with a mean, a scandalous design to prey upon your fortune.

[32]See William W. Appleton, "The Double Gallant in Eighteenth-Century Comedy," in *English Writers of the Eighteenth Century*, ed. John H. Middendorf (New York, 1971), pp. 145–46, 149. Appleton, who accepts the traditional view of Restoration comedy as Hobbesian and sentimental comedy as Shaftesburian and sees Archer and Aimwell as representative of the two philosophies, makes clear that Farquhar was not alone in employing this device of the paired heroes.

> But the beauties of your mind and person have so won me
> from myself that like a trusty servant I prefer the interest of
> my mistress to my own.
>
> (V.iv.20–33)

The character of Mrs. Sullen, like that of Archer, has its roots in the Restoration comedy of manners; in the frankness of her language and in the acknowledgment of her physical desires, Mrs. Sullen resembles the traditional female rake. But she is a rake with a difference. In the first place, nothing comes of her rakish talk; and, in the second, she is a character for whom we are to have at least some real concern. Much of her loose talk, as she admits to Dorinda, is just that:

> It happens with us, as among the men, the greatest talkers
> are the greatest cowards; and there's a reason for it: those
> spirits evaporate in prattle which might do more mischief if
> they took another course.
>
> (IV.i.454–58)

In contrast, the setting (the country rather than London) and the increased importance of the lower (and even disreputable) classes turn *The Beaux' Stratagem* toward the increasingly bourgeois future rather than toward the aristocratic past, where one would never have been exposed so extensively to servants, innkeepers, countrywomen, and highwaymen, nor to the details of domestic management revealed both at Lady Bountiful's house and at Boniface's inn. And the future that *The Beaux' Stratagem* faces is not so much that of sentimental comedy—such as Cibber's *The Careless Husband* (1704), Steele's *The Conscious Lovers* (1722), or the weeping comedies of Cumberland—but rather that of the more astringent and entertaining works of Oliver Goldsmith and Richard Brinsley Sheridan. Farquhar's comedy shares much with Goldsmith's *She Stoops to Conquer* (1773), not only lively humor and appealing characters but also the use of characters belonging to the gentry disguised as servants in order to achieve their goals. As in Sheridan's *The School for Scandal* (1777), there is much talk about sex with very little in the way of practical results[33]—though Mrs. Sullen is in greater danger of succumbing to temptation than is Lady Teazle. Farquhar has been accused of killing the comedy of manners, but he can just as justifiably be credited with fathering (or grandfathering) the kind of comedy that later came from the pens of Goldsmith and Sheridan.[34]

The disagreement over what *The Beaux' Stratagem* is about, over what values, if any, it espouses, is, however, of more importance than that over defining the kind of comedy it is. Until the twentieth century, most commentators assumed that it was simply an entertainment, morally reprehensible to some, morally neutral to others. In the earlier years of this century, it was generally considered, along with the rest of Restoration comedy, as a kind of social document, a source of information about eighteenth-century society, its customs and manners. It is only fairly recently that *The Beaux' Stratagem* has been examined as a work based on and expressing ideas related to the nature of man and his society and presenting moral conclusions resulting from an evaluation of those ideas.[35] It has been seen as illustrating the conflict between rational social laws and passion,[36] or that between natural law and

---

[33]The avoidance of adultery and fornication in their plays was not, of course, new with Farquhar and Sheridan.

[34]Allardyce Nicoll makes a distinction between the comedy of Goldsmith and that of Sheridan. The former writer, he says, believed that sentimental comedy was too genteel, that it eliminated real nature and humor. Therefore, Goldsmith wished to return to Shakespeare where these elements resided in abundance. Sheridan, on the other hand, looked back only as far as Congreve, and it was his intention to restore real wit to the stage (*A History of the English Drama,* 3:158). These are valid distinctions insofar as Goldsmith's and Sheridan's intentions are concerned; yet the worlds of the two writers are very much the same in the effect on readers and audiences. And the world of *The Beaux' Stratagem*, full as it is of nature, wit, and humor, affects us in much the same way.

[35]Norman N. Holland's chapter, "The Critical Failure," in *The First Modern Comedies* (Bloomington, Ind., 1959), pp. 199–209, provides a useful survey of the development of the criticism of Restoration comedy.

[36]Ronald Berman, "The Comedy of Reason," *Texas Studies in Literature and Language* 7 (1965): 161–68, finds in the play an unresolved conflict between a rational social order based on the principles of commerce (each character seems to know just how much each person or each action is worth, and "the final cause of the play [is] the sum of ten thousand pounds" [p. 161]) and individual passions (Aimwell's, for instance) which

artificial social rules;[37] it has been considered as an exploration of various ways of seeking pleasure,[38] as a statement of the difficulty, if not impossibility, of maintaining satisfactory human relationships, particularly in marriage,[39] and, at least in part, as a metaphorical analysis of human motives.[40] Whether or not one accepts the possibility that all of these themes are present in *The Beaux' Stratagem* to a greater or lesser degree (a tenable position, it seems to me), one must acknowledge that Farquhar is concerned, at least tangentially, with serious social ideas and problems.

Whatever forces are in conflict, that there is conflict in the play is made manifest by the way in which Farquhar sets up pairs of characters, settings, ideas. There are two settings, the inn and Lady Bountiful's house. The values attached to these settings are in opposition: at the inn, highwaymen plot crimes, London beaux plot stratagems, a father attempts to corrupt his daughter, money is stolen, and drunkenness is encouraged; at Lady Bountiful's, charity and concern for others dominate, the sick are made well, the wicked converted to virtue. Lady Bountiful's world is invaded by, but manages to overcome in one way or another, external antagonistic forces. Robbers break in to steal material goods;

---

prevail in the end, seemingly rejecting "the whole scheme by which the play has operated" (p. 168).

[37]Eric Rothstein argues both in *George Farquhar* (New York, 1967), pp. 148–58, and in his edition of *The Beaux' Stratagem* (New York, 1967), pp. xii–xvii, that the play is based on the canons of Natural Law as they were known in the seventeenth and eighteenth centuries. These laws, expressed most explicitly in the passages based on Milton but alluded to elsewhere in the play, govern every human activity and relationship, and it is the opposition to them of unnatural or diseased forces (individual or institutional) that sets up the basic conflict of the play.

[38]Garland Jack Gravitt, "A Primer of Pleasure: Neo-Epicureanism in Farquhar's *The Beaux Stratagem*," *Thoth* 12, no. 2 (1972): 38–49, sees the play as one in which every character is searching for pleasure in either acceptable or unacceptable ways (those based on reason and those not so based).

[39]William L. Sharp, "Restoration Comedy: An Approach to Modern Production," *Drama Survey*, 7, nos. 1 and 2 (Winter, 1968–69), pp. 69–86.

[40]"What Farquhar gives us in *The Beaux' Stratagem*," argues Alan Roper, "is a play notable for a conspicuous . . . integrity of action, character, dialogue, and setting. By making the moral world of his play commensurate with fully realized places, he is closer, for all the lesser comprehensiveness and intensity of his imagination, to Shakespeare and Jonson than he is to Congreve and Etherege" ("*The Beaux' Stratagem*: Image and Action," in *Seventeenth-Century Imagery*, ed. Earl Miner [Berkeley, 1971], pp. 177–78).

gentlemen, more or less in disguise, insinuate themselves under false pretenses to steal not only money (Dorinda's fortune) but also female virtue (Mrs. Sullen's). That the highwaymen and the beaux are equated is made obvious by Farquhar when he describes Gibbet, Aimwell, and Archer all as younger sons forced to make their own way in the world. (Gay was later to make good use of this equation of the upper classes and the underworld in *The Beggar's Opera*.)

The forces invading Lady Bountiful's household come from the traditionally corrupt town. Aimwell and Archer are from London; the highwaymen prey on travelers coming from or going to London; the inn, while in the provinces, is on the main road to London; and the persons who stop there are generally on their way from one town to another. These corrupt forces are eventually either overcome and made impotent or transformed by the country values associated with Lady Bountiful.[41] It is worth noting that in each setting there is at least one character who would seem more at home in the other. Gipsy is a corrupt and corrupting element (consider her relationship with Foigard and her willingness to admit alien elements into the house) at Lady Bountiful's, whereas Cherry remains uncorrupted at the inn and in fact is partly responsible for overcoming the corrupting forces. It would seem to be no coincidence that at the end of the play Cherry is to replace Gipsy in Dorinda's service.

Other features that suggest Farquhar's concerns include a considerable attention paid to such concepts as freedom, particularly in its negative aspects. Count Bellair is a prisoner of war, bound to good behavior by his word; Mrs. Sullen is a prisoner of her marriage, an institution she refers to in terms of shackles, chains, and yokes. Aimwell's and Archer's situation is limited, their actions constrained, by their lack of money; they are, in a sense, prisoners of their poverty. Gibbet and his men, if not incarcerated, are always in danger of being so, as is Foigard because of his employ-

---

[41]There are a number of lighthearted conversations on the subject of town versus country. Aimwell and Archer are agreed in praising London and its delights, whereas Mrs. Sullen and Dorinda argue over the relative merits of town and country; Mrs. Sullen is particularly contemptuous of "country pleasures." For a discussion of this subject in its context, see John Loftis, *Comedy and Society from Congreve to Fielding* (Stanford, Calif., 1959), pp. 72–74.

ment by an enemy nation. One could argue that Sullen is a prisoner of his own brutish limitations. Almost everyone is restrained or imprisoned in some way, and certain conclusions can be reached about Farquhar's views on the characters and the values they represent by recognizing who is free and who is not, and why, at the end.

Many have pointed out the importance of money and financial themes in *The Beaux' Stratagem* (much traditional comedy deals, at least on the surface, with attempts, honest and dishonest, to acquire or to retain fortunes, one's own or others'). Everything, and everyone, is discussed with reference to worth and price. One value is exchanged for another. Aimwell and Archer have spent one fortune and are now on the prowl for another. Gipsy performs favors (in several senses) in exchange for money. Sullen expects someone to buy back his wife; for him her person is a liability but her fortune an asset that he intends to keep. Much is made of Dorinda's fortune, and even she sees it as a useful part of herself; and when she "loses" it to Archer and it goes to her brother in exchange for his wife, she receives ample compensation in her marriage to Aimwell. Finally, Mrs. Sullen is practically auctioned off, being bought back from her husband by Archer with Dorinda's fortune. Money can be considered as both a good and an evil; certainly its lack limits some of the characters, and its possession frees them to act according to their desires. But is one to assume that everyone who gains a fortune at the end of the play deserves it, that somehow wealth is the proper reward for virtuous behavior, forced or voluntary? Or are there ambiguities that Farquhar wants us to see in these situations so that we can recognize that life's system of rewards and punishments is not simple? Or is he merely making use of his society's view of material goods, displaying his characters within a system that his audience recognizes as a given of its society?

Similar questions are raised by the way in which other themes or concepts emerge during the course of the play. Much is made of the contrast between truly human behavior (Lady Bountiful, for instance) and animal-like behavior (Sullen). Archer contrasts unfavorably the "inhumane wretches" who "by sacrificing all to one appetite . . . starve all the rest" to the "man that keeps his five senses keen and bright as his sword." Closely related to this theme is the recurrent appearance of the contrast between the physical and the mental, most noticeable in Mrs. Sullen's comments on her husband and in her brother's conversation with Sullen and Boniface at the inn (note his "Mr. Guts" speech). One can make much or little of these subjects, but Farquhar does at least seem to raise the questions.

One theme evident to all is that based on Milton's ideas on marriage and divorce, although not everyone agrees about the seriousness with which Farquhar presents these ideas. It is generally assumed now that, although Farquhar did not intend to reform Britain's divorce laws, he was seriously concerned about them and the harm they did to mismatched couples.[42] We are clearly not intended simply to laugh at and then dismiss the extreme incompatability between the Sullens, particularly since Mrs. Sullen is given characteristics that make her an appealing and relatively complex individual. Her distaste for and boredom with "country pleasures" are not merely the result of her being a superficial citified female; they are part of the frustration resulting from having to cope with an almost totally unresponsive husband, a husband who represents the cruder country pleasures. Clearly she is wasted on him, even though she may not be what Milton had in mind when he described the ideal marriage; her interests are too physical, her goals too exclusively pleasure-oriented. We do not see her as an intellectual creature, potentially the helpmeet of some eighteenth-century Miltonic gentleman; but then Milton's ideals are impracticably high, and he was never as interested in the problem of the mismatched wife as he was in that of the mismatched husband. Farquhar is not trying to illustrate Milton's principles on the level Milton expresses them; he employs them on a lower and more practical level. Incompatability is incompatability no matter where on the social or intellectual (or sexual) scale. And Sullen's bestiality is without doubt several cuts below Mrs. Sullen's sensuous nature.

[42]Rothstein asserts that Milton's ideas are used by Farquhar simply "as support for the rather ambiguous conduct of Mrs. Sullen and Sir Charles Freeman. The characters do not express, but rather shelter beneath, the moral and legal umbrella of Milton's principles" (*Beaux' Stratagem*, p. ix). V. F. Hopper and G. B. Lahey in their edition of the play (Great Neck, N.Y., 1963) seem to agree (pp. 38–41). It is possible that they all underestimate at least the seriousness of Farquhar's concern, though one can agree that he is certainly not a reforming activist.

The extreme contrast established between Mrs. Sullen and her husband is not the only way in which Farquhar attracts the audience to her. The wit she employs in her exchanges with Dorinda and others, the brave and frequently ironic view she has of her own situation, increase our sympathy for her, especially when she is brought up short by a reminder of reality. After the two women have viewed the paintings with Aimwell and Archer, each tries to outdo the other in descriptions of the flattery they have received from the gentlemen. Mrs. Sullen clearly tops Dorinda in the exchange until the latter fantasizes about marriage with Lord Aimwell. Then the contrast is too much for Mrs. Sullen, and she weeps. This is the only time she seems to be overcome by her situation, and the contrast to her usual bravery is exceptionally poignant. Even her whimsical treatment of the countrywoman, which on the surface may seem unfeeling, can be seen as the desperate action of a frustrated woman driven by serious problems.

All this is not to suggest that Mrs. Sullen is a tragedy queen who has found her way by mistake into a comedy. The overall tone of the play is witty and humorous enough to counteract or balance the genuinely serious element in Mrs. Sullen and her situation. That one is moved without being depressed seems to me evidence that Farquhar has succeeded in integrating what might have been disparate elements, and in so doing he has given what might have been a trivial comedy an impressive weight. He has made it a portion of reality that reveals his serious concern about real problems.

Farquhar's concern about the marriage issue seems all the more real because he does not present an ideal marriage as a model, nor does he pretend to solve the problems he describes. Mrs. Sullen is freed from the burden of her husband's company, she has regained her fortune, but she is not free to marry. It would take an act of Parliament to separate her legally from her husband, and very few such acts were passed before divorce laws were finally liberalized in the nineteenth century. She has a choice between a kind of spinsterhood and a kind of whoredom.

Even her relationship with Archer seems unlikely to continue. Although many critics have assumed that Mrs. Sullen is freed from her husband for the purpose of having an adulterous affair with Archer[43]—a solution that would certainly trivialize the nature of Farquhar's concern—there is little evidence in the play to support such a conclusion. Archer does agree to pay Mrs. Sullen's portion, but only in a manner of speaking; the documents that he has from Sullen's writing desk make payment unnecessary. And it is Mrs. Sullen's own fortune that Archer returns to her brother, Sir Charles. So he is not out of pocket as a result of his "generosity"; and since he has just been promised Dorinda's fortune of ten thousand pounds by Aimwell, he has no need for an alliance with a wealthy woman.

Certainly Archer and Mrs. Sullen are not in love. Both of them throughout the play consciously play games, games that might have ended in an affair at one time. But Archer's real interest is obviously in Cherry; when he hears that the inn has been robbed and the money is gone, he says, "Rot the money! My wench is gone"; and it is he who arranges for Cherry to be in Dorinda's service, where he will presumably have access to her.

Mrs. Sullen's situation has been palliated sufficiently so that the comedy seems to end happily. Aimwell and Dorinda, the conventional and not very interesting young lovers, may perhaps live very happily forever after; Archer, now that he has his fortune, may very well continue the life of the rake and never feel the need for a permanent relationship. But on reflection, when the play is over, we recognize that Mrs. Sullen's lot is the clearest and the saddest; she is not really as free as the final couplet of the play blithely suggests she is,[44] and we have a certain amount of sym-

---

[43]Like Mrs. Oldfield, G. S. Alleman, in *Matrimonial Law and the Materials of Restoration Comedy* (Wallingford, Pa., 1942), which describes the actual laws existing at this time, assumes that "the heroine goes off into justifiable adultery" (p. 107). But one can hardly read Archer's request for "Your hand" before the dance as a proposal, decent or indecent, of marriage. It is significant that the penultimate couplet of the play refers to the joining of Dorinda and Aimwell and the separation of the Sullens, but not to the joining of Archer and Mrs. Sullen.

[44]It is not possible to take the final couplet literally, since it does not reflect accurately the situation that has gone before: "Consent, if mutual, saves the lawyer's fee;/ Consent is law enough to set you free." In the first place, the consent is hardly mutual; Mr. Sullen has had no real choice. And the freedom is a limited kind of freedom, since, though both of them are free of each other's company, neither is free to marry another—a much greater disadvantage to her than to him. The couplet, then, is a kind of glib equivalent of the storybook ending for Aimwell and Dorinda, something we can accept temporarily so long as we give it no real thought.

pathy and compassion for the character who reminds us that life is more difficult and complex than we might wish it to be.

I should like to thank the many friends and colleagues who have assisted me during the preparation of this edition, especially George Dekker, the late Claude M. Simpson, and, most especially, David Rodes. Previous editors of *The Beaux' Stratagem* have put me deeply in their debt, as have the many librarians in Great Britain and the United States who have answered my questions and provided me with microfilm and photocopy. And to my wife, who has devoted many hours to this project, I am, as always, deeply grateful.

CHARLES N. FIFER

Stanford University

THE BEAUX' STRATAGEM

ADVERTISEMENT

The reader may find some faults in this play, which my
illness prevented the amending of; but there is great
amends made in the representation, which cannot be
matched, no more than the friendly and indefatigable
care of Mr. Wilks, to whom I chiefly owe the success of   5
the play.

GEORGE FARQUHAR

---

4. *Mr. Wilks*] Robert Wilks (ca. 1665–1732), actor, manager, and inti-
mate friend of Farquhar, to whom the playwright left the care of his
children. He created the roles of Captain Plume in Farquhar's *The Recruiting Officer* and Archer in *The Beaux' Stratagem*.

PROLOGUE

Spoken by Mr. Wilks

When strife disturbs or sloth corrupts an age,
Keen satire is the business of the stage.
When the Plain-Dealer writ, he lashed those crimes
Which then infested most—the modish times.
But now, when faction sleeps and sloth is fled,   5
And all our youth in active fields are bred;
When through Great Britain's fair extensive round,
The trumps of fame the notes of Union sound;
When Anna's scepter points the laws their course,
And her example gives her precepts force,   10
There scarce is room for satire; all our lays
Must be or songs of triumph or of praise.
But as in grounds best cultivated, tares
And poppies rise among the golden ears,
Our products so, fit for the field or school,   15
Must mix with nature's favorite plant—a fool.
A weed that has to twenty summers ran,
Shoots up in stalk and vegetates to man.
Simpling our author goes from field to field
And culls such fools as may diversion yield;   20
And, thanks to nature, there's no want of those,
For rain, or shine, the thriving coxcomb grows.
Follies, tonight we show, ne'er lashed before,
Yet, such as Nature shows you every hour;
Nor can the pictures give a just offense,   25
For fools are made for jests to men of sense.

---

3. *Plain-Dealer*] William Wycherley (1641–1715), whose comedy of that name was first produced probably on 11 December 1676.

6. *active fields*] England and France were at war from 1702 to 1713 (War of the Spanish Succession).

8. *Union*] The bill for the union of England and Scotland received the royal assent on 6 March 1707, two days before the play was first produced. The Union took effect on 1 May.

19. *Simpling*] "To seek for, or gather, simples, or medicinal herbs" (OED, which cites this passage).

20. *culls*] selects, chooses.

DRAMATIS PERSONAE

Men

AIMWELL	two gentlemen of broken fortunes, the first as master, and the second	Mr. *Mills*
ARCHER	as servant	Mr. *Wilks*

COUNT BELLAIR, a French officer, prisoner at Lichfield — Mr. *Bowman*

SULLEN, a country blockhead, brutal to his wife — Mr. *Verbruggen*

FREEMAN, a gentleman from London — Mr. *Keen*

FOIGARD, a priest, chaplain to the French officers — Mr. *Bowen*

GIBBET, a highway man — Mr. *Cibber*

HOUNSLOW
BAGSHOT } his companions

BONIFACE, landlord of the inn — Mr. *Bullock*

SCRUB, servant to Mr. Sullen — Mr. *Norris*

Women

LADY BOUNTIFUL, an old civil country gentlewoman, that cures all her neighbors of all distempers, and foolishly fond of her son Sullen — Mrs. *Powell*

DORINDA, Lady Bountiful's daughter — Mrs. *Bradshaw*

MRS. SULLEN, her daughter-in-law — Mrs. *Oldfield*

GIPSY, maid to the ladies — Mrs. *Mills*

CHERRY, the landlord's daughter in the inn — Mrs. *Bicknell*

Scene: *Lichfield*

Additional characters not listed in the Dramatis Personae are a Tapster, a Servant, a Fellow, and a Countrywoman.

THE BEAUX' STRATAGEM

ACT I

Scene: an inn.
Enter Boniface *running.*

BONIFACE.

Chamberlain, maid, Cherry, daughter Cherry! All
asleep, all dead?

Enter Cherry *running.*

CHERRY.

Here, here, why d'ye bawl so, father? D'ye think we have
no ears?

BONIFACE.

You deserve to have none, you young minx. The com-   5
pany of the Warrington coach has stood in the hall this
hour, and nobody to show them to their chambers.

CHERRY.

And let 'em wait farther; there's neither redcoat in the
coach nor footman behind it.

BONIFACE.

But they threaten to go to another inn tonight.   10

CHERRY.

That they dare not for fear the coachman should over-
turn them tomorrow. —Coming, coming. —Here's the
London coach arrived.

ACT I] *Q2;* ACT I. SCENE I *Q1.*   8. wait farther] *Q1;* wait, father *W2*
and many later eds.

---

1. *Chamberlain*] servant in charge of bedrooms at the inn.
6. *Warrington coach*] Warrington is a town about sixty miles northwest of
Lichfield. As late as 1797, passengers traveling from London to Liverpool
made a dinner stop of thirty-five minutes at Lichfield before going on to
Warrington and then Liverpool (Edmund Vale, *The Mail Coach Men of the
Late Eighteenth Century* [London, 1960], p. 239).

Enter several people with trunks, bandboxes, and other luggage, and cross the stage.

BONIFACE.

Welcome, ladies.

CHERRY.

Very welcome, gentlemen. —Chamberlain, show the   15
Lion and the Rose.   *Exit with the company.*

Enter Aimwell *in riding habit,* Archer *as footman carrying a portman-tle.*

BONIFACE.

This way, this way, gentlemen.

AIMWELL.

Set down the things, go to the stable, and see my horses
well rubbed.

ARCHER.

I shall, sir.   *Exit.*   20

AIMWELL.

You're my landlord, I suppose?

BONIFACE.

Yes, sir, I'm old Will Boniface, pretty well known upon
this road, as the saying is.

AIMWELL.

O, Mr. Boniface, your servant.

BONIFACE.

O, sir, what will your honor please to drink, as the saying   25
is?

AIMWELL.

I have heard your town of Lichfield much famed for ale.
I think I'll taste that.

BONIFACE.

Sir, I have now in my cellar ten tun of the best ale in
Staffordshire; 'tis smooth as oil, sweet as milk, clear as   30
amber, and strong as brandy, and will be just fourteen

15–16. *the Lion and the Rose*] rooms in the inn.

16.1–2. *portmantle*] another form, common in the eighteenth century,
of "portmanteau" (OED: "a case or bag for carrying clothing and other
necessaries when travelling").

29. *tun*] a cask holding over two hundred gallons of wine.

year old the fifth day of next March old style.

AIMWELL.

You're very exact, I find, in the age of your ale.

BONIFACE.

As punctual, sir, as I am in the age of my children. I'll
show you such ale— Here, tapster, broach Number   35
1706, as the saying is. —Sir, you shall taste my Anno
Domini. I have lived in Lichfield man and boy above
eight and fifty years and, I believe, have not consumed
eight and fifty ounces of meat.

AIMWELL.

At a meal, you mean, if one may guess your sense by   40
your bulk.

BONIFACE.

Not in my life, sir. I have fed purely upon ale. I have eat
my ale, drank my ale, and I always sleep upon ale.

Enter Tapster *with a bottle and glass.*

Now, sir, you shall see. (*Filling it out.*) Your worship's
health. Ha, delicious, delicious! Fancy it Burgundy, only   45
fancy it, and 'tis worth ten shillings a quart.

AIMWELL (*drinks*).

'Tis confounded strong.

BONIFACE.

Strong! It must be so, or how should we be strong that
drink it?

AIMWELL.

And have you lived so long upon this ale, landlord?   50

BONIFACE.

Eight and fifty years, upon my credit, sir, but it killed my
wife, poor woman, as the saying is.

---

32. *old style*] according to the Julian Calendar. Pope Gregory XIII cor-
rected the calendar in 1582, but Britain did not adopt the Gregorian
Calendar (new style) until 1752, when the old calendar was eleven days
behind that used by the rest of Europe.

35–36. *Number 1706*] signifying the ale of 1706? If so, it is hardly fourteen years old, as Boniface claims.

43.1. *glass*] Since Boniface later drinks with Aimwell, the tapster (as
William Archer notes in his edition) must bring two glasses, into both of
which Boniface pours wine.

44. *S.D. Filling it out*] pouring it out.

AIMWELL.

How came that to pass?

BONIFACE.

I don't know how, sir. She would not let the ale take its
natural course, sir; she was for qualifying it every now   55
and then with a dram, as the saying is. And an honest
gentleman that came this way from Ireland made her a
present of a dozen bottles of usquebaugh, but the poor
woman was never well after. But howe'er, I was obliged
to the gentleman, you know.   60

AIMWELL.

Why, was it the usquebaugh that killed her?

BONIFACE.

My Lady Bountiful said so. She, good lady, did what
could be done: she cured her of three tympanies, but
the fourth carried her off. But she's happy, and I'm
contented, as the saying is.   65

AIMWELL.

Who's that Lady Bountiful you mentioned?

BONIFACE.

'Ods my life, sir, we'll drink her health. (*Drinks.*) My
Lady Bountiful is one of the best of women. Her last
husband, Sir Charles Bountiful, left her worth a
thousand pound a year, and I believe she lays out one   70
half on't in charitable uses for the good of her
neighbors. She cures rheumatisms, ruptures, and bro-
ken shins in men; green sickness, obstructions, and fits
of the mother in women; the king's evil, chin-cough, and
chilblains in children. In short, she has cured more   75
people in and about Lichfield within ten years than the
doctors have killed in twenty, and that's a bold word.

---

58. *usquebaugh*] whiskey. *OED* cites this passage.

63. *tympanies*] distention of the abdomen caused by gas or air in the
intestine or uterus; sometimes loosely used for swelling or tumors of any
kind. *OED* cites this passage.

73. *green sickness*] chlorosis, a form of anemia primarily affecting adoles-
cent girls.

73–74. *fits of the mother*] hysteria. *OED* cites this passage.

74. *the king's evil*] scrofula, supposed to be cured by the king's touch.
Queen Anne was the last English monarch to perform this service.

74. *chin-cough*] whooping cough.

AIMWELL.

Has the lady been any other way useful in her generation?

BONIFACE.

Yes, sir, she has a daughter by Sir Charles, the finest   80
woman in all our country, and the greatest fortune. She
has a son too by her first husband, Squire Sullen, who
married a fine lady from London t'other day. If you
please, sir, we'll drink his health?

AIMWELL.

What sort of a man is he?   85

BONIFACE.

Why, sir, the man's well enough, says little, thinks less,
and does—nothing at all, faith. But he's a man of a great
estate and values nobody.

AIMWELL.

A sportsman, I suppose?

BONIFACE.

Yes, sir, he's a man of pleasure: he plays at whisk and   90
smokes his pipe eight and forty hours together sometimes.

AIMWELL.

And married, you say?

BONIFACE.

Ay, and to a curious woman, sir. But he's a—he wants it
here, sir.   *Pointing to his forehead.*   95

AIMWELL.

He has it there, you mean.

BONIFACE.

That's none of my business; he's my landlord, and so a
man, you know, would not—but—Icod, he's no better
than—sir, my humble service to you. (*Drinks*.)
Though I value not a farthing what he can do to me. I   100

---

90. *whisk*] an earlier name for the card game, very much like bridge,
now called whist.

94–96. *he wants . . . you mean*] Boniface suggests that Sullen is mentally
deficient. Aimwell implies that Sullen wears cuckold's horns.

98. *Icod*] a variant of "ecod" or "egad," a mild asseveration or oath like
"i'faith" or "by God."

pay him his rent at quarter day, I have a good running
trade, I have but one daughter, and I can give her— but
no matter for that.

AIMWELL.

You're very happy, Mr. Boniface. Pray, what other
company have you in town?   105

BONIFACE.

A power of fine ladies, and then we have the French
officers.

AIMWELL.

O, that's right; you have a good many of those gentlemen. Pray, how do you like their company?

BONIFACE.

So well, as the saying is, that I could wish we had as 110
many more of 'em. They're full of money and pay double for everything they have. They know, sir, that we
paid good round taxes for the taking of 'em, and so they
are willing to reimburse us a little. One of 'em lodges in
my house.   115

Enter Archer.

ARCHER.

Landlord, there are some French gentlemen below that
ask for you.

BONIFACE.

I'll wait on 'em. —([*Aside*] *to* Archer.)   Does your master
stay long in town, as the saying is?

ARCHER.

I can't tell, as the saying is.   120

BONIFACE.

Come from London?

ARCHER.

No.

BONIFACE.

Going to London, mayhap?

ARCHER.

No.

---

101. *quarter day*] one of the four days (25 March, 24 June, 29 September,
and 25 December) on which payment of rent and other quarterly charges
fall due.

106–7. *French officers*] prisoners of war who lived on parole in country
towns. Lichfield was one of the parole towns throughout the eighteenth
century.

BONIFACE.

>An odd fellow this. —[*To* Aimwell.] I beg your wor- 125
>ship's pardon. I'll wait on you in half a minute. *Exit.*

AIMWELL.

>The coast's clear, I see. Now, my dear Archer, welcome
>to Lichfield.

ARCHER.

>I thank thee, my dear brother in iniquity.

AIMWELL.

>Iniquity! Prithee leave canting. You need not change 130
>your style with your dress.

ARCHER.

>Don't mistake me, Aimwell, for 'tis still my maxim that
>there is no scandal like rags nor any crime so shameful
>as poverty.

AIMWELL.

>The world confesses it every day in its practice though 135
>men won't own it for their opinion. Who did that worthy
>lord, my brother, single out of the side-box to sup with
>him t'other night?

ARCHER.

>Jack Handycraft, a handsome, well dressed, mannerly,
>sharping rogue, who keeps the best company in town. 140

AIMWELL.

>Right; and pray who married my Lady Manslaughter
>t'other day, the great fortune?

ARCHER.

>Why, Nick Marrabone, a professed pickpocket and a
>good bowler, but he makes a handsome figure and rides

---

130. *canting*] speaking hypocritically or piously.

137. *side-box*] box at the side of the theater where fashionable people often sat when they were more interested in being seen than in watching the play.

143. *Marrabone*] thought to be a corruption of "Marylebone," at this time still a small village on the outskirts of London where no doubt many pickpockets plied their trade at the Marylebone Gardens, a popular place of entertainment. The surrounding fields, often used by duelists, were noted for harboring robbers.

143–44. *a good bowler*] an ironical twist of the proverbial "honest man and a good bowler." Cf., for example, "He is a marvellous good neighbor, faith, and a very good bowler" (*Love's Labor's Lost*, V.ii.584) and "The vulgar Proverb's crost, he hardly can be a good Bowler and an Honest Man" (Quarles's *Emblemes* 1.10). *OED* cites this passage.

in his coach that he formerly used to ride behind.   145

AIMWELL.

But did you observe poor Jack Generous in the park last
week?

ARCHER.

Yes, with his autumnal periwig shading his melancholy
face, his coat older than anything but its fashion, with
one hand idle in his pocket and with the other picking   150
his useless teeth; and though the Mall was crowded with
company, yet was poor Jack as single and solitary as a
lion in a desert.

AIMWELL.

And as much avoided for no crime upon earth but the
want of money.   155

ARCHER.

And that's enough. Men must not be poor; idleness is
the root of all evil; the world's wide enough, let 'em
bustle. Fortune has taken the weak under her protection, but men of sense are left to their industry.

AIMWELL.

Upon which topic we proceed, and I think luckily   160
hitherto. Would not any man swear now that I am a man
of quality and you my servant, when if our intrinsic
value were known—

ARCHER.

Come, come, we are the men of intrinsic value who can
strike our fortunes out of ourselves, whose worth is in-   165
dependent of accidents in life or revolutions in government. We have heads to get money and hearts to spend
it.

AIMWELL.

As to our hearts, I grant ye, they are as willing tits as any
within twenty degrees, but I can have no great opinion   170
of our heads from the service they have done us
hitherto, unless it be that they have brought us from
London hither to Lichfield, made me a lord and you my
servant.

169. *tits*] small or scrawny horses, nags.
170. *twenty degrees*] degrees of latitude or longitude.

ARCHER.

That's more than you could expect already. But what 175
money have we left?

AIMWELL.

But two hundred pound.

ARCHER.

And our horses, clothes, rings, etc. Why we have very
good fortunes now for moderate people; and let me tell
you, besides, that this two hundred pound, with the ex- 180
perience that we are now masters of, is a better estate
than the ten thousand we have spent. Our friends indeed began to suspect that our pockets were low, but we
came off with flying colors, showed no signs of want
either in word or deed.   185

AIMWELL.

Ay, and our going to Brussels was a good pretense
enough for our sudden disappearing; and I warrant you
our friends imagine that we are gone a-volunteering.

ARCHER.

Why, faith, if this prospect fails, it must e'en come to
that. I am for venturing one of the hundreds, if you will, 190
upon this knight-errantry, but in case it should fail, we'll
reserve the other to carry us to some counterscarp
where we may die as we lived, in a blaze.

AIMWELL.

With all my heart. And we have lived justly, Archer; we
can't say that we have spent our fortunes, but that we 195
have enjoyed 'em.

ARCHER.

Right; so much pleasure for so much money. We have
had our pennyworths, and had I millions, I would go to
the same market again. O, London, London! Well, we

180. you, besides, that] *O;* you, be-   182. ten thousand we] *O;* ten we
sides thousand, that *Q1.*   *Q1.*
                                            192. the other] *W2;* the t'other *Q1.*

186. *Brussels*] one of the cities taken by the English and their allies in the
previous year. There had been considerable military activity in almost the
whole of Flanders and Brabant.
    192. *counterscarp*] a kind of fortification: "the outer wall or slope of the
ditch, which supports the covered way" (*OED*).

have had our share, and let us be thankful. Past plea- 200
sures, for aught I know, are best, such as we are sure of;
those to come may disappoint us.

AIMWELL.

It has often grieved the heart of me to see how some
inhumane wretches murther their kind fortunes, those
that by sacrificing all to one appetite shall starve all the 205
rest. You shall have some that live only in their palates,
and in their sense of tasting shall drown the other four.
Others are only epicures in appearances, such who shall
starve their nights to make a figure a-days and famish
their own to feed the eyes of others. A contrary sort 210
confine their pleasures to the dark and contract their
spacious acres to the circuit of a muff-string.

ARCHER.

Right, but they find the Indies in that spot where they
consume 'em, and I think your kind keepers have much
the best on't, for they indulge the most senses by one 215
expense; there's the seeing, hearing, and feeling amply
gratified, and some philosophers will tell you that from
such a commerce there arises a sixth sense that gives
infinitely more pleasure than the other five put together.   220

AIMWELL.

And to pass to the other extremity, of all keepers I think
those the worst that keep their money.

ARCHER.

Those are the most miserable wights in being; they destroy the rights of nature and disappoint the blessings of
providence. Give me a man that keeps his five senses 225
keen and bright as his sword, that has 'em always drawn
out in their just order and strength, with his reason as
commander at the head of 'em, that detaches 'em by
turns upon whatever party of pleasure agreeably offers,
and commands 'em to retreat upon the least appearance 230
of disadvantage or danger. For my part, I can stick to
my bottle, while my wine, my company, and my reason

---

214. *kind keepers*] keepers of mistresses.
223. *wights*] creatures, men.

holds good; I can be charmed with Sappho's singing
without falling in love with her face; I love hunting, but
would not, like Actaeon, be eaten up by my own dogs; 235
I love a fine house, but let another keep it; and just so I
love a fine woman.

AIMWELL.

In that last particular you have the better of me.

ARCHER.

Ay, you're such an amorous puppy that I'm afraid
you'll spoil our sport. You can't counterfeit the passion 240
without feeling it.

AIMWELL.

Though the whining part be out of doors in town, 'tis
still in force with the country ladies. And let me tell you,
Frank, the fool in that passion shall outdo the knave at
any time.   245

ARCHER.

Well, I won't dispute it now. You command for the day,
and so I submit. At Nottingham, you know, I am to be
master.

AIMWELL.

And at Lincoln, I again.

ARCHER.

Then at Norwich I mount, which, I think, shall be our 250
last stage, for if we fail there we'll embark for Holland,
bid adieu to Venus, and welcome Mars.

AIMWELL.

A match!

Enter Boniface.

Mum.

BONIFACE.

What will your worship please to have for supper?   255

---

233. *Sappho*] Greek lyric poetess born on the island of Lesbos sometime
near the middle of the seventh century B.C.

235. *Actaeon*] in Greek mythology, the hunter who saw Artemis bathing.
She changed him into a stag, and he was killed by his own dogs.

242. *the whining part*] "If a man should make love in an ordinary tone,
his mistress would not regard him; and therefore he must whine"(*OED*,
quoting Selden's *Table Talk*).

242. *out of doors*] clearly meaning "out of date" or "out of fashion," but
OED gives no such meaning.

AIMWELL.

What have you got?

BONIFACE.

Sir, we have a delicate piece of beef in the pot and a pig at the fire.

AIMWELL.

Good supper meat, I must confess. I can't eat beef, landlord.   260

ARCHER.

And I hate pig.

AIMWELL.

Hold your prating, sirrah, do you know who you are?

BONIFACE.

Please to bespeak something else. I have everything in the house.

AIMWELL.

Have you any veal?   265

BONIFACE.

Veal! Sir, we had a delicate loin of veal on Wednesday last.

AIMWELL.

Have you got any fish or wildfowl?

BONIFACE.

As for fish, truly, sir, we are an inland town and indifferently provided with fish, that's the truth on't. And 270 then for wildfowl—we have a delicate couple of rabbits.

AIMWELL.

Get me the rabbits fricasseed.

BONIFACE.

Fricasseed! Lard, sir, they'll eat much better smothered with onions.

ARCHER.

Pshaw, damn your onions!   275

AIMWELL.

Again, sirrah! —Well, landlord, what you please. But hold, I have a small charge of money, and your house is so full of strangers that I believe it may be safer in your

---

272. *fricassed*] sliced, fried, or stewed, and served with a sauce.

277. *charge*] amount, although the word suggests a burden or a responsibility.

custody than mine, for when this fellow of mine gets
drunk, he minds nothing. —Here, sirrah, reach me the   280
strongbox.

ARCHER.
Yes, sir. —(*Aside*.) This will give us a reputation.
                                              Brings the box.

AIMWELL.
Here, landlord, the locks are sealed down both for your
security and mine; it holds somewhat above two
hundred pound. If you doubt it, I'll count it to you after   285
supper. But be sure you lay it where I may have it at a
minute's warning, for my affairs are a little dubious at
present. Perhaps I may be gone in half an hour; perhaps
I may be your guest till the best part of that be spent.
And pray order your ostler to keep my horses always   290
saddled. But one thing above the rest I must beg, that
you would let this fellow have none of your Anno Domini, as you call it, for he's the most insufferable sot.
—Here, sirrah, light me to my chamber.
                                              Exit lighted by Archer.

BONIFACE.
Cherry, daughter Cherry?   295

                    Enter Cherry.

CHERRY.
D'ye call, father?

BONIFACE.
Ay, child, you must lay by this box for the gentleman; 'tis
full of money.

CHERRY.
Money, all that money! Why, sure, father, the gentleman comes to be chosen Parliament-man. Who is he?   300

BONIFACE.
I don't know what to make of him. He talks of keeping
his horses ready saddled and of going perhaps at a min-

---

290. *ostler*] a stableman or groom. The spelling represents the pronun-
ciation of "hostler" with *h* mute.
    300. *Parliament-man*] Candidates for Parliament often bribed the elec-
tors.

ute's warning, or of staying perhaps till the best part of
this be spent.

CHERRY.

Ay, ten to one, father, he's a highwayman.   305

BONIFACE.

A highwayman! Upon my life, girl, you have hit it, and
this box is some new-purchased booty. Now could we
find him out, the money were ours.

CHERRY.

He don't belong to our gang.

BONIFACE.

What horses have they?   310

CHERRY.

The master rides upon a black.

BONIFACE.

A black! Ten to one the man upon the black mare, and
since he don't belong to our fraternity, we may betray
him with a safe conscience. I don't think it lawful to
harbor any rogues but my own. Look ye, child, as the   315
saying is, we must go cunningly to work. Proofs we must
have. The gentleman's servant loves drink: I'll ply him
that way; and ten to one loves a wench: you must work
him t'other way.

CHERRY.

Father, would you have me give my secret for his?   320

BONIFACE.

Consider, child, there's two hundred pound to boot.
—(*Ringing without.*) Coming, coming. —Child, mind
your business.

CHERRY.

What a rogue is my father! My father! I deny it. My
mother was a good, generous, free-hearted woman, and   325
I can't tell how far her good nature might have extended for the good of her children. This landlord of
mine, for I think I can call him no more, would betray
his guest and debauch his daughter into the bargain—by
a footman, too!   330

Enter Archer.

ARCHER.

What footman, pray, mistress, is so happy as to be the subject of your contemplation?

CHERRY.

Whoever he is, friend, he'll be but little the better for't.

ARCHER.

I hope so, for I'm sure you did not think of me.

CHERRY.

Suppose I had?   335

ARCHER.

Why then you're but even with me, for the minute I came in I was a-considering in what manner I should make love to you.

CHERRY.

Love to me, friend!

ARCHER.

Yes, child.   340

CHERRY.

Child! Manners. If you kept a little more distance, friend, it would become you much better.

ARCHER.

Distance! Good night, saucebox.   *Going.*

CHERRY.

A pretty fellow! I like his pride. —Sir, pray, sir, you see, sir (Archer *returns*), I have the credit to be intrusted with 345 your master's fortune here, which sets me a degree above his footman. I hope, sir, you an't affronted.

ARCHER.

Let me look you full in the face, and I'll tell you whether you can affront me or no. S'death, child, you have a pair of delicate eyes, and you don't know what to do with 350 'em.

CHERRY.

Why, sir, don't I see everybody?

ARCHER.

Ay, but if some women had 'em they would kill everybody. Prithee, instruct me; I would fain make love to you, but I don't know what to say.   355

CHERRY.

Why, did you never make love to anybody before?

ARCHER.

Never to a person of your figure. I can assure you,
madam, my addresses have been always confined to
people within my own sphere. I never aspired so high
before.　　　　　　　　　　　　　　　　　　　　　360

A Song.

But you look so bright,
And are dressed so tight
That a man would swear you're right
As arm was e'er laid over.

Such an air　　　　　　　　　　　　　　　　　365
You freely wear
To ensnare
As makes each guest a lover.

Since then, my dear, I'm your guest,
Prithee give me of the best　　　　　　　　　370
Of what is ready dressed.
Since then, my dear, etc.

CHERRY (*aside*).

What can I think of this man? —Will you give me that
song, sir?

ARCHER.

Ay, my dear, take it while 'tis warm. (*Kisses her.*) Death　375
and fire, her lips are honeycombs!

CHERRY.

And I wish there had been bees, too, to have stung you
for your impudence.

ARCHER.

There's a swarm of Cupids, my little Venus, that has
done the business much better.　　　　　　　　380

CHERRY (*aside*).

This fellow is misbegotten as well as I. —What's your
name, sir?

ARCHER (*aside*).

Name! Igad, I have forgot it. —Oh! Martin.

361–72. But you . . . my dear, etc.]　*century eds. print only the first two*
W6; Q1–2 *and many other 18th–*　*lines, followed by "A Song."*

CHERRY.
  Where were you born?
ARCHER.
  In St. Martin's parish.   385
CHERRY.
  What was your father?
ARCHER.
  St. Martin's Parish.
CHERRY.
  Then, friend, good night.
ARCHER.
  I hope not.
CHERRY.
  You may depend upon't.   390
ARCHER.
  Upon what?
CHERRY.
  That you're very impudent.
ARCHER.
  That you're very handsome.
CHERRY.
  That you're a footman.
ARCHER.
  That you're an angel.   395
CHERRY.
  I shall be rude.
ARCHER.
  So shall I.
CHERRY.
  Let go my hand.
ARCHER.
  Give me a kiss.   *Kisses her.*

                    Call without, Cherry, Cherry.

CHERRY.
  I'mm—my father calls. You plaguy devil, how durst 400
  you stop my breath so? Offer to follow me one step, if
  you dare.   [*Exit* Cherry.]
ARCHER.
  A fair challenge, by this light. This is a pretty fair open-

ing of an adventure, but we are knight-errants, and so
fortune be our guide. *Exit.* 405

End of the First Act.

ACT II

Scene: *A gallery in Lady Bountiful's house.*
            [Enter] Mrs. Sullen *and* Dorinda *meeting.*

DORINDA.

Morrow, my dear sister, are you for church this morning?

MRS. SULLEN.

Anywhere to pray, for heaven alone can help me. But I
think, Dorinda, there's no form of prayer in the liturgy
against bad husbands.   5

DORINDA.

But there's a form of law in Doctors' Commons, and I
swear, Sister Sullen, rather than see you thus continually
discontented I would advise you to apply to that. For
besides the part that I bear in your vexatious broils, as
being sister to the husband and friend to the wife, your   10
example gives me such an impression of matrimony that
I shall be apt to condemn my person to a long vaca-
tion all its life. But supposing, madam, that you brought it
to a case of separation, what can you urge against your
husband? My brother is, first, the most constant man   15
alive.

MRS. SULLEN.

The most constant husband, I grant ye.

DORINDA.

He never sleeps from you.

MRS. SULLEN.

No, he always sleeps with me.

DORINDA.

He allows you a maintenance suitable to your quality.   20

MRS. SULLEN.

A maintenance! Do you take me, madam, for an hospital
child, that I must sit down and bless my benefactors for

---

6. *Doctors' Commons*] the College of Doctors of Civil Law in London
which dealt with ecclesiastical law, divorce suits, marriage licenses, and
wills. The society was dissolved in 1858.
21–22. *hospital child*] a foundling.

meat, drink, and clothes? As I take it, madam, I brought
your brother ten thousand pounds, out of which I might
expect some pretty things called pleasures.   25
DORINDA.
You share in all the pleasures that the country affords.
MRS. SULLEN.
Country pleasures! Racks and torments! Dost think,
child, that my limbs were made for leaping of ditches
and clambering over stiles; or that my parents, wisely
foreseeing my future happiness in country pleasures,   30
had early instructed me in the rural accomplishments of
drinking fat ale, playing at whisk, and smoking tobacco
with my husband; or of spreading of plasters, brewing
of diet drinks, and stilling rosemary water with the good
old gentlewoman, my mother-in-law?   35
DORINDA.
I'm sorry, madam, that it is not more in our power to
divert you. I could wish indeed that our entertainments
were a little more polite or your taste a little less refined.
But pray, madam, how came the poets and philosophers
that labored so much in hunting after pleasure to place   40
it at last in a country life?
MRS. SULLEN.
Because they wanted money, child, to find out the pleasures of the town. Did you ever see a poet or philoso-
pher worth ten thousand pound? If you can show me
such a man, I'll lay you fifty pound you'll find him   45
somewhere within the weekly bills. Not that I disap-
prove rural pleasures as the poets have painted them;

---

32. *fat ale*] fruity, full-bodied ale.
34. *stilling*] distilling. *OED* cites this passage.
34. *rosemary water*] made from the rosemary, a fragrant evergreen
shrub. It has a pungent bitterish taste and, besides being used in phar-
maceutical preparations, is an ingredient in soaps, colognes, and hair
lotions.
46. *weekly bills*] the official list of deaths (and later, births) published
since 1592 by the London Company of Parish Clerks. The parishes covered by this list (originally 109 in number) were considered to be "within
the bills of mortality."

in their landscape every Phyllis has her Corydon, every
murmuring stream and every flowery mead gives fresh
alarms to love. Besides, you'll find that their couples   50
were never married. But yonder I see my Corydon, and
a sweet swain it is, heaven knows. Come, Dorinda, don't
be angry. He's my husband and your brother, and between both is he not a sad brute?

DORINDA.
I have nothing to say to your part of him; you're the best   55
judge.

MRS. SULLEN.
O, sister, sister, if ever you marry, beware of a sullen,
silent sot, one that's always musing but never thinks.
There's some diversion in a talking blockhead, and since
a woman must wear chains, I would have the pleasure of   60
hearing 'em rattle a little. Now you shall see, but take
this by the way. He came home this morning at his usual
hour of four, wakened me out of a sweet dream of
something else by tumbling over the tea table, which he
broke all to pieces. After his man and he had rolled   65
about the room like sick passengers in a storm, he comes
flounce into bed, dead as a salmon into a fishmonger's
basket, his feet cold as ice, his breath hot as a furnace,
and his hands and his face as greasy as his flannel nightcap. Oh matrimony! He tosses up the clothes with a   70
barbarous swing over his shoulders, disorders the whole
economy of my bed, leaves me half naked, and my
whole night's comfort is the tuneable serenade of that
wakeful nightingale, his nose. O, the pleasure of count-
ing the melancholy clock by a snoring husband! But   75
now, sister, you shall see how handsomely, being a well-
bred man, he will beg my pardon.

Enter Sullen.

---

48. *Phyllis* . . . *Corydon*] traditional names for shepherdesses and
shepherds in pastoral poetry.
70. *clothes*] bedclothes.
72. *economy*] order, arrangement.

SULLEN.

My head aches consumedly.

MRS. SULLEN.

Will you be pleased, my dear, to drink tea with us this
morning? It may do your head good.   80

SULLEN.

No.

DORINDA.

Coffee, brother?

SULLEN.

Pshaw.

MRS. SULLEN.

Will you please to dress and go to church with me? The
air may help you.   85

SULLEN.

Scrub.

Enter Scrub.

SCRUB.

Sir?

SULLEN.

What day o'th' week is this?

SCRUB.

Sunday, an't please your worship.

SULLEN.

Sunday! Bring me a dram, and, d'ye hear, set out the   90
venison-pasty and a tankard of strong beer upon the
hall table. I'll go to breakfast.   *Going.*

DORINDA.

Stay, stay, brother, you shan't get off so. You were very
naught last night and must make your wife reparation.
Come, come, brother, won't you ask pardon?   95

SULLEN.

For what?

DORINDA.

For being drunk last night.

SULLEN.

I can afford it, can't I?

---

94. *naught*] an early form of "naughty."

MRS. SULLEN.
> But I can't, sir.

SULLEN.
> Then you may let it alone.   100

MRS. SULLEN.
> But I must tell you, sir, that this is not to be borne.

SULLEN.
> I'm glad on't.

MRS. SULLEN.
> What is the reason, sir, that you use me thus in-
> humanely?

SULLEN.
> Scrub.   105

SCRUB.
> Sir?

SULLEN.
> Get things ready to shave my head.   *Exit.*

MRS. SULLEN.
> Have a care of coming near his temples, Scrub, for fear
> you meet something there that may turn the edge of
> your razor.   *Exit* Scrub. 110
> Inveterate stupidity! Did you ever know so hard, so obs-
> tinate a spleen as his? O, sister, sister, I shall never ha'
> good of the beast till I get him to town. London, dear
> London, is the place for managing and breaking a hus-
> band.   115

DORINDA.
> And has not a husband the same opportunities there for
> humbling a wife?

MRS. SULLEN.
> No, no, child, 'tis a standing maxim in conjugal disci-
> pline that when a man would enslave his wife he hurries
> her into the country, and when a lady would be arbitrary 120
> with her husband she wheedles her booby up to town. A
> man dare not play the tyrant in London because there
> are so many examples to encourage the subject to rebel.
> O, Dorinda, Dorinda, a fine woman may do anything in

---

107. *shave my head*] Men kept their heads shaved under their wigs.
112. *spleen*] bad temper.

London. O' my conscience, she may raise an army of 125
forty thousand men.

DORINDA.

I fancy, sister, you have a mind to be trying your power
that way here in Lichfield; you have drawn the French
count to your colors already.

MRS. SULLEN.

The French are a people that can't live without their 130
gallantries.

DORINDA.

And some English that I know, sister, are not averse to
such amusements.

MRS. SULLEN.

Well, sister, since the truth must out, it may do as well
now as hereafter. I think one way to rouse my lethargic 135
sottish husband is to give him a rival. Security begets
negligence in all people, and men must be alarmed to
make 'em alert in their duty. Women are like pictures of
no value in the hands of a fool till he hears men of sense
bid high for the purchase.   140

DORINDA.

This might do, sister, if my brother's understanding
were to be convinced into a passion for you, but I fancy
there's a natural aversion of his side. And I fancy, sister,
that you don't come much behind him, if you dealt
fairly.   145

MRS. SULLEN.

I own it. We are united contradictions, fire and water.
But I could be contented, with a great many other wives,
to humor the censorious mob and give the world an
appearance of living well with my husband, could I
bring him but to dissemble a little kindness to keep me 150
in countenance.

DORINDA.

But how do you know, sister, but that instead of rousing
your husband by this artifice to a counterfeit kindness,
he should awake in a real fury?

MRS. SULLEN.

Let him. If I can't entice him to the one, I would pro- 155
voke him to the other.

DORINDA.

But how must I behave myself between ye?

MRS. SULLEN.

You must assist me.

DORINDA.

What, against my own brother?

MRS. SULLEN.

He's but half a brother, and I'm your entire friend. If I   160
go a step beyond the bounds of honor, leave me; till
then I expect you should go along with me in everything. While I trust my honor in your hands, you may
trust your brother's in mine. The count is to dine here
today.   165

DORINDA.

'Tis a strange thing, sister, that I can't like that man.

MRS. SULLEN.

You like nothing; your time is not come. Love and death
have their fatalities and strike home one time or other.
You'll pay for all one day, I warrant ye. But, come, my
lady's tea is ready, and 'tis almost church time.   170

Exeunt.

[II.ii]   *Scene: the inn.*
Enter Aimwell, *dressed, and* Archer.

AIMWELL.

And was she the daughter of the house?

ARCHER.

The landlord is so blind as to think so, but I dare swear
she has better blood in her veins.

AIMWELL.

Why dost think so?

ARCHER.

Because the baggage has a pert *je ne sais quoi*. She reads   5
plays, keeps a monkey, and is troubled with vapors.

---

5. *je ne sais quoi*] an indescribable or inexpressible quality; literally "I
know not what."

5–6. *She* . . . *vapors*] traditional activities of a woman of fashion. To
suffer from the vapors was to be subject to hypochondria, depression, or
other neurotic ailments.

AIMWELL.

By which discoveries I guess that you know more of her.

ARCHER.

Not yet, faith. The lady gives herself airs, forsooth; nothing under a gentleman.

AIMWELL.

Let me take her in hand.   10

ARCHER.

Say one word more o' that, and I'll declare myself, spoil your sport there, and everywhere else. Look ye, Aimwell, every man in his own sphere.

AIMWELL.

Right, and therefore you must pimp for your master.

ARCHER.

In the usual forms, good sir, after I have served myself.   15
But to our business. You are so well dressed, Tom, and make so handsome a figure that I fancy you may do execution in a country church. The exterior part strikes first, and you're in the right to make that impression favorable.   20

AIMWELL.

There's something in that which may turn to advantage. The appearance of a stranger in a country church draws as many gazers as a blazing star. No sooner he comes into the cathedral but a train of whispers runs buzzing round the congregation in a moment: "Who is he?   25
Whence comes he? Do you know him?" Then I, sir, tips me the verger with half a crown. He pockets the simony and inducts me into the best pew in the church. I pull out my snuffbox, turn myself round, bow to the bishop—or the dean, if he be the commanding officer—single   30
gle out a beauty, rivet both my eyes to hers, set my nose a-bleeding by the strength of imagination, and show the whole church my concern by my endeavoring to hide it. After the sermon the whole town gives me to her for a

---

23. *blazing star*] comet.

27. *verger*] usher.

27. *simony*] buying or selling ecclesiastical preferments. *OED*, seeming to ignore the humor, notes that Farquhar's use of the word to mean "tip" is both obsolete and rare.

lover, and by persuading the lady that I am a-dying for   35
her, the tables are turned, and she in good earnest falls
in love with me.

ARCHER.

There's nothing in this, Tom, without a precedent. But
instead of riveting your eyes to a beauty, try to fix 'em
upon a fortune; that's our business at present.   40

AIMWELL.

Pshaw, no woman can be a beauty without a fortune. Let
me alone, for I am a marksman.

ARCHER.

Tom.

AIMWELL.

Ay.

ARCHER.

When were you at church before, pray?   45

AIMWELL.

Um—I was there at the coronation.

ARCHER.

And how can you expect a blessing by going to church
now?

AIMWELL.

Blessing! Nay, Frank, I ask but for a wife.   *Exit.*

ARCHER.

Truly the man is not very unreasonable in his demands.   50
                              Exit at the opposite door.

Enter Boniface *and* Cherry.

BONIFACE.

Well, daughter, as the saying is, have you brought Martin to confess?

CHERRY.

Pray, father, don't put me upon getting anything out of
a man. I'm but young, you know, father, and I don't
understand wheedling.   55

BONIFACE.

Young! Why you jade, as the saying is, can any woman
wheedle that is not young? Your mother was useless at

---

46. *coronation*] the coronation of Queen Anne on 23 April 1702.

five and twenty. Not wheedle! Would you make your
mother a whore and me a cuckold, as the saying is? I tell
you his silence confesses it, and his master spends his   60
money so freely and is so much a gentleman every manner of way that he must be a highwayman.

Enter Gibbet *in a cloak.*

GIBBET.

Landlord, landlord, is the coast clear?

BONIFACE.

O, Mr. Gibbet, what's the news?

GIBBET.

No matter, ask no questions, all fair and honorable.   65
Here, my dear Cherry (*gives her a bag*), two hundred
sterling pounds as good as any that ever hanged or
saved a rogue; lay 'em by with the rest. And here—three
wedding or mourning rings, 'tis much the same, you
know. Here, two silver-hilted swords; I took those from   70
fellows that never show any part of their swords but the
hilts. Here is a diamond necklace which the lady hid in
the privatest place in the coach, but I found it out. This
gold watch I took from a pawnbroker's wife. It was left
in her hands by a person of quality; there's the arms   75
upon the case.

CHERRY.

But who had you the money from?

GIBBET.

Ah, poor woman! I pitied her. From a poor lady just
eloped from her husband. She had made up her cargo
and was bound for Ireland as hard as she could drive.   80
She told me of her husband's barbarous usage, and so I
left her half a crown. But I had almost forgot, my dear
Cherry, I have a present for you.

CHERRY.

What is't?

58. Not wheedle!] *Q1; om. C5.*

69. *mourning rings*] rings worn in memory of a dead person. Money to
pay for a ring was frequently bequeathed to friends in the will of the
deceased.

GIBBET.

A pot of cereuse, my child, that I took out of a lady's   85
under-pocket.

CHERRY.

What, Mr. Gibbet, do you think that I paint?

GIBBET.

Why, you jade, your betters do. I'm sure the lady that I
took it from had a coronet upon her handkerchief.
Here, take my cloak, and go secure the premises.   90

CHERRY.

I will secure 'em.   *Exit.*

BONIFACE.

But, hark ye, where's Hounslow and Bagshot?

GIBBET.

They'll be here tonight.

BONIFACE.

D'ye know of any other gentlemen o' the pad on this
road?   95

GIBBET.

No.

BONIFACE.

I fancy that I have two that lodge in the house just now.

GIBBET.

The devil! How d'ye smoke 'em?

BONIFACE.

Why, the one is gone to church.

GIBBET.

That's suspicious, I must confess.   100

BONIFACE.

And the other is now in his master's chamber; he pre-
tends to be servant to the other. We'll call him out and
pump him a little.

GIBBET.

With all my heart.

---

85. *cereuse*] a cosmetic made of white lead.

90. *premises*] the previously-mentioned articles. The humor of Gibbet's
use of the word lies in the fact that it is a legal term.

94. *gentlemen o'the pad*] highwaymen. "Pad," meaning path or road, came
originally from vagabonds' slang. *OED* cites this passage.

98. *smoke*] find out about, suspect, have a notion of.

BONIFACE.

Mr. Martin, Mr. Martin.   105

Enter Martin [Archer] *combing a periwig, and singing.*

GIBBET.

The roads are consumed deep; I'm as dirty as old
Brentford at Christmas. A good pretty fellow that.
—Whose servant are you, friend?

ARCHER.

My master's.

GIBBET.

Really?   110

ARCHER.

Really.

GIBBET.

That's much. The fellow has been at the bar, by his
evasions. —But, pray, sir, what is your master's name?

ARCHER.

Tall, all dall. (*Sings and combs the periwig.*) This is the
most obstinate curl.   115

GIBBET.

I ask you his name.

ARCHER.

Name, sir,—tall, all dall—I never asked him his name in
my life. Tall, all dall.

BONIFACE.

What think you now?

GIBBET.

Plain, plain, he talks now as if he were before a judge. 120
—But, pray, friend, which way does your master travel?

ARCHER.

A-horseback.

106–7. *dirty as old Brentford*] In winter, Brentford's High Street, a part of
the Great West Road, was often under eight or nine inches of mud. The
mud was as much as a foot and a half deep on either side of the central
track.

112. *at the bar*] in court; originally the bar was simply "the barrier or
wooden rail marking off the immediate precinct of the judge's seat, at
which prisoners are stationed for arraignment, trial, or sentence" (*OED*).

GIBBET.

Very well again, an old offender, right. —But I mean
does he go upwards or downwards?

ARCHER.

Downwards, I fear, sir. Tall, all.   125

GIBBET.

I'm afraid my fate will be a contrary way.

BONIFACE.

Ha, ha, ha! Mr. Martin, you're very arch. This gentleman is only traveling towards Chester and would be glad
of your company, that's all. —Come, captain, you'll stay
tonight, I suppose. I'll show you a chamber. Come, cap- 130
tain.

GIBBET.

Farewell, friend.   *Exit* [*with* Boniface].

ARCHER.

Captain, your servant. —Captain! a pretty fellow.
S'death, I wonder that the officers of the army don't
conspire to beat all scoundrels in red but their own.   135

Enter Cherry.

CHERRY (*aside*).

Gone, and Martin here! I hope he did not listen. I would
have the merit of the discovery all my own because I
would oblige him to love me. —Mr. Martin, who was
that man with my father?

ARCHER.

Some recruiting sergeant or whipped-out trooper, I   140
suppose.

CHERRY.

All's safe, I find.

ARCHER.

Come, my dear, have you conned over the catechize I
taught you last night?

---

124. *upwards or downwards*] toward London or away from it.
125. *Downwards*] no doubt financially or socially downwards.
126. *a contrary way*] that is, he will be hanged.
140. *whipped-out trooper*] Some offenses required whipping in addition to
a dishonorable discharge from the army.
143. *catechize*] short for "catechism," a series of questions (often of a
religious nature) with official, correct answers.

CHERRY.

    Come, question me.   145

ARCHER.

    What is love?

CHERRY.

    Love is I know not what, it comes I know not how, and
goes I know not when.

ARCHER.

    Very well; an apt scholar.   *Chucks her under the chin.*

    Where does love enter?   150

CHERRY.

    Into the eyes.

ARCHER.

    And where go out?

CHERRY.

    I won't tell ye.

ARCHER.

    What are the objects of that passion?

CHERRY.

    Youth, beauty, and clean linen.   155

ARCHER.

    The reason?

CHERRY.

    The two first are fashionable in nature and the third at
court.

ARCHER.

    That's my dear. What are the signs and tokens of that
passion?   160

CHERRY.

    A stealing look, a stammering tongue, words improba-
ble, designs impossible, and actions impracticable.

ARCHER.

    That's my good child. Kiss me. What must a lover do to
obtain his mistress?

CHERRY.

    He must adore the person that disdains him. He must 165
bribe the chambermaid that betrays him and court the
footman that laughs at him. He must, he must—

ARCHER.

    Nay, child, I must whip you if you don't mind your

lesson. He must treat his—

CHERRY.

O, ay, he must treat his enemies with respect, his friends 170
with indifference, and all the world with contempt. He
must suffer much and fear more. He must desire much
and hope little. In short, he must embrace his ruin and
throw himself away.

ARCHER.

Had ever man so hopeful a pupil as mine? Come, my 175
dear, why is love called a riddle?

CHERRY.

Because, being blind, he leads those that see, and
though a child he governs a man.

ARCHER.

Mighty well. And why is love pictured blind?

CHERRY.

Because the painters out of the weakness or privilege of 180
their art chose to hide those eyes that they could not
draw.

ARCHER.

That's my dear little scholar. Kiss me again. And why
should love, that's a child, govern a man?

CHERRY.

Because that a child is the end of love.   185

ARCHER.

And so ends love's catechism. And now, my dear, we'll
go in and make my master's bed.

CHERRY.

Hold, hold, Mr. Martin. You have taken a great deal of
pains to instruct me, and what d'ye think I have learnt
by it?   190

ARCHER.

What?

CHERRY.

That your discourse and your habit are contradictions,
and it would be nonsense in me to believe you a footman
any longer.

ARCHER.

'Oons, what a witch it is!   195

---

195. *'Oons*] a contraction of "God's wounds," an oath.

CHERRY.

Depend upon this, sir, nothing in this garb shall ever
tempt me, for though I was born to servitude, I hate it.
Own your condition, swear you love me, and then—

ARCHER.

And then we shall go make the bed.

CHERRY.

Yes.   200

ARCHER.

You must know then that I am born a gentleman. My
education was liberal, but I went to London a younger
brother, fell into the hands of sharpers who stripped me
of my money. My friends disowned me, and now my
necessity brings me to what you see.   205

CHERRY.

Then take my hands, promise to marry me before you
sleep, and I'll make you master of two thousand pound.

ARCHER.

How!

CHERRY.

Two thousand pound that I have this minute in my own
custody; so throw off your livery this instant, and I'll go   210
find a parson.

ARCHER.

What said you? A parson!

CHERRY.

What, do you scruple?

ARCHER.

Scruple, no, no, but—two thousand pound you say?

CHERRY.

And better.   215

ARCHER.

S'death, what shall I do? But hark'ee, child, what need
you make me master of yourself and money when you
may have the same pleasure out of me and still keep
your fortune in your hands?

CHERRY.

Then you won't marry me?   220

219. your hands] *Q1;* your own
hands *W6.*

ARCHER.

I would marry you, but—

CHERRY.

O, sweet sir, I'm your humble servant. You're fairly
caught. Would you persuade me that any gentleman
who could bear the scandal of wearing a livery would
refuse two thousand pound, let the condition be what it   225
would? No, no, sir. But I hope you'll pardon the freedom I have taken, since it was only to inform myself of
the respect that I ought to pay you.   *Going.*

ARCHER.

Fairly bit, by Jupiter. —Hold, hold, and have you actu-
ally two thousand pound?   230

CHERRY.

Sir, I have my secrets as well as you. When you please to
be more open I shall be more free, and be assured that I
have discoveries that will match yours, be what they will.
In the meanwhile be satisfied that no discovery I make
shall ever hurt you, but beware of my father.   235

                                    [*Exit* Cherry.]

ARCHER.

So, we're like to have as many adventures in our inn as
Don Quixote had in his. Let me see—two thousand
pound! If the wench would promise to die when the
money were spent, Igad, one would marry her, but the
fortune may go off in a year or two, and the wife may   240
live—Lord knows how long? Then an innkeeper's
daughter—ay, that's the devil. There my pride brings
me off.

    For whatsoe'er the sages charge on pride,
    The angels' fall, and twenty faults beside;   245
    On earth I'm sure, 'mong us of mortal calling,
    Pride saves man oft, and woman too, from falling.

                                          Exit.

End of the Second Act.

222. O, sweet sir] *C;* O sweet, sir
Q1.

ACT III

[III.i]   *Scene: Lady Bountiful's house.*
       Enter Mrs. Sullen, Dorinda.

MRS. SULLEN.

Ha, ha, ha, my dear sister, let me embrace thee. Now we
are friends indeed, for I shall have a secret of yours as a
pledge for mine. Now you'll be good for something: I
shall have you conversable in the subjects of the sex.

DORINDA.

But do you think that I am so weak as to fall in love with 5
a fellow at first sight?

MRS. SULLEN.

Pshaw, now you spoil all. Why should not we be as free
in our friendships as the men? I warrant you the gentleman has got to his confidant already, has avowed his
passion, toasted your health, called you ten thousand 10
angels, has run over your lips, eyes, neck, shape, air, and
everything, in a description that warms their mirth to a
second enjoyment.

DORINDA.

Your hand, sister. I an't well.

MRS. SULLEN [*aside*].

So, she's breeding already. —Come, child, up with it 15
—hem a little—so—now tell me, don't you like the gentleman that we saw at church just now?

DORINDA.

The man's well enough.

MRS. SULLEN.

Well enough! Is he not a demigod, a Narcissus, a star,
the man i'the moon?   20

0.2. *Scene: Lady Bountiful's house*] *gallery in Lady Bountiful's house. O.
D1; Scene continues Q1; Scene: the*

---

19. *Narcissus*] the beautiful son of the river god Cephissus and the
nymph Liriope, who fell in love with his own reflection in a pool and was
changed to the flower bearing his name.

DORINDA.

O, sister, I'm extremely ill.

MRS. SULLEN.

Shall I send to your mother, child, for a little of her
cephalic plaster to put to the soles of your feet, or shall I
send to the gentleman for something for you? Come,
unlace your stays; unbosom yourself. The man is per-   25
fectly a pretty fellow. I saw him when he first came into
church.

DORINDA.

I saw him too, sister, and with an air that shone,
methought, like rays about his person.

MRS. SULLEN.

Well said; up with it.   30

DORINDA.

No forward coquette behavior, no airs to set him off, no
studied looks nor artful posture, but nature did it all.

MRS. SULLEN.

Better and better. One touch more, come.

DORINDA.

But then his looks—did you observe his eyes?

MRS. SULLEN.

Yes, yes, I did. His eyes, well, what of his eyes?   35

DORINDA.

Sprightly, but not wandering; they seemed to view but
never gazed on anything but me. And then his looks so
humble were, and yet so noble, that they aimed to tell
me that he could with pride die at my feet though he
scorned slavery anywhere else.   40

MRS. SULLEN.

The physic works purely! How d'ye find yourself now,
my dear?

DORINDA.

Hem, much better, my dear. O, here comes our Mercury.

---

23. *cephalic plaster*] a plaster supposed to cure or relieve disorders of the
head. *OED* cites this passage.

41. *physic*] medicine.

43–44. *Mercury*] messenger. Mercury was the messenger and herald of
the gods.

Enter Scrub.

Well, Scrub, what news of the gentleman?   45
SCRUB.

Madam, I have brought you a packet of news.
DORINDA.

Open it quickly, come.
SCRUB.

In the first place I enquired who the gentleman was;
they told me he was a stranger. Secondly, I asked what
the gentleman was; they answered and said that they   50
never saw him before. Thirdly, I enquired what countryman he was; they replied 'twas more than they knew.
Fourthly, I demanded whence he came; their answer
was, they could not tell. And fifthly, I asked whither he
went, and they replied they knew nothing of the matter. 55
And this is all I could learn.
MRS. SULLEN.

But what do the people say? Can't they guess?
SCRUB.

Why, some think he's a spy, some guess he's a mountebank, some say one thing, some another; but for my
own part I believe he's a Jesuit.   60
DORINDA.

A Jesuit! Why a Jesuit?
SCRUB.

Because he keeps his horses always ready saddled, and
his footman talks French.
MRS. SULLEN.

His footman!
SCRUB.

Ay, he and the count's footman were gabbering French 65
like two intriguing ducks in a millpond, and I believe
they talked of me, for they laughed consumedly.
DORINDA.

What sort of livery has the footman?
SCRUB.

Livery! Lord, madam, I took him for a captain, he's so

58–59. *mountebank*] a quack, cheat, or charlatan.
65. *gabbering*] an obsolete form of "jabbering."

bedizened with lace. And then he has tops to his shoes 70
up to his mid-leg, a silver-headed cane dangling at his
knuckles. He carries his hands in his pockets just so
(*walks in the French air*) and has a fine long periwig tied
up in a bag. Lord, Madam, he's clear another sort of
man than I. 75

MRS. SULLEN.
That may easily be. —But what shall we do now, sister?

DORINDA.
I have it. This fellow has a world of simplicity and some
cunning; the first hides the latter by abundance.
—Scrub.

SCRUB.
Madam. 80

DORINDA.
We have a great mind to know who this gentleman is,
only for our satisfaction.

SCRUB.
Yes, madam, it would be a satisfaction, no doubt.

DORINDA.
You must go and ·get acquainted with his footman and
invite him hither to drink a bottle of your ale because 85
you're butler today.

SCRUB.
Yes, madam, I am butler every Sunday.

MRS. SULLEN.
O brave, sister! O' my conscience, you understand the
mathematics already. 'Tis the best plot in the world.
Your mother, you know, will be gone to church, my 90
spouse will be got to the alehouse with his scoundrels,
and the house will be our own; so we drop in by accident
and ask the fellow some questions ourselves. In the
country, you know, any stranger is company, and we're
glad to take up with the butler in a country dance and 95
happy if he'll do us the favor.

SCRUB.
O, madam, you wrong me. I never refused your ladyship the favor in my life.

---

74. *bag*] a silk pouch used to hold up the back hair of a wig.

Enter Gipsy.

GIPSY.

Ladies, dinner's upon table.

DORINDA.

Scrub, we'll excuse your waiting. Go where we ordered 100
you.

SCRUB.

I shall. *Exeunt.*

[III.ii] *Scene changes to the inn.*
Enter Aimwell *and* Archer.

ARCHER.

Well, Tom, I find you're a marksman.

AIMWELL.

A marksman! Who so blind could be as not discern a
swan among the ravens?

ARCHER.

Well, but heark'ee, Aimwell.

AIMWELL.

Aimwell! Call me Oroondates, Cesario, Amadis, all that 5
romance can in a lover paint, and then I'll answer. O,
Archer, I read her thousands in her looks. She looked
like Ceres in her harvest: corn, wine and oil, milk and
honey, gardens, groves, and purling streams played on
her plenteous face. 10

ARCHER.

Her face! Her pocket, you mean; the corn, wine and oil
lies there. In short, she has ten thousand pound; that's
the English on't.

AIMWELL.

Her eyes—

ARCHER.

Are demicannons, to be sure, so I won't stand their bat- 15
tery. *Going.*

---

5. *Oroondates, Cesario, Amadis*] heroic characters of prose romances (respectively La Calprenède's *Cassandre* and *Cléopâtre,* and the Spanish or
Portuguese *Amadis de Gaula* as written by García de Montalvo, all published in English translations).

15. *demicannons*] cannons having a bore of about six and a half inches.
The balls weighed from thirty to thirty-six pounds.

AIMWELL.
>   Pray excuse me; my passion must have vent.

ARCHER.
>   Passion! What a plague! D'ye think these romantic airs
>   will do our business? Were my temper as extravagant as
>   yours my adventures have something more romantic by   20
>   half.

AIMWELL.
>   Your adventures!

ARCHER.
>   Yes,
>   The nymph that with her twice ten hundred pounds
>   With brazen engine hot, and coif clear starched   25
>   Can fire the guest in warming of the bed—
>   There's a touch of sublime Milton for you, and the sub-
>   ject but an innkeeper's daughter. I can play with a girl as
>   an angler does with his fish: he keeps it at the end of his
>   line, runs it up the stream and down the stream, till at   30
>   last he brings it to hand, tickles the trout, and so whips it
>   into his basket.

Enter Boniface.

BONIFACE.
>   Mr. Martin, as the saying is, yonder's an honest fellow
>   below, my Lady Bountiful's butler, who begs the honor
>   that you would go home with him and see his cellar.   35

ARCHER.
>   Do my *baisemains* to the gentleman, and tell him I will do
>   myself the honor to wait on him immediately.

>   *Exit* Boniface.

---

18. D'ye] *Q2;* D'ee *Q1.*   ship's commands, as the saying is.
37.1.   Exit   Boniface]   *Q1;*   *Exit, bowing obsequiously. W6.*
BONIFACE. I shall do your wor-

---

25. *brazen engine*] warming pan.
25. *coif*] a close-fitting, hood-like cap.
27. *a touch . . . Milton*] Parodies of Milton were extremely popular in the
eighteenth century. These lines are singularly un-Miltonic.
31. *tickles the trout*] captures the trout by reaching for it with the hands
and sliding the fingers into its gills.
36. *baisemains*] compliments, respects; literally "a kiss of the hands."
OED cites this passage.

AIMWELL.

What do I hear—soft Orpheus play and fair Toftida sing?

ARCHER.

Pshaw, damn your raptures! I tell you here's a pump 40
going to be put into the vessel, and the ship will get into
harbor, my life on't. You say there's another lady very
handsome there?

AIMWELL.

Yes, faith.

ARCHER.

I'm in love with her already.   45

AIMWELL.

Can't you give me a bill upon Cherry in the meantime?

ARCHER.

No, no, friend, all her corn, wine, and oil is engrossed to
my market. And once more I warn you to keep your
anchorage clear of mine, for if you fall foul of me, by
this light you shall go to the bottom. What, make prize of 50
my little frigate while I am upon the cruise for you?   *Exit.*

Enter Boniface.

AIMWELL.

Well, well, I won't. —Landlord, have you any tolerable
company in the house? I don't care for dining alone.

BONIFACE.

Yes, sir, there's a captain below, as the saying is, that
arrived about an hour ago.   55

AIMWELL.

Gentlemen of his coat are welcome everywhere. Will you
make him a compliment from me and tell him I should
be glad of his company.

45. I'm] *Q2;* I'am *Q1.*

---

38. *Orpheus*] son of the muse Calliope, who played the lyre so skillfully
that wild beasts were spellbound.
38. *Toftida*] Katherine Tofts (d. 1756), famous soprano, the first English
singer to perform Italian opera in England.
46. *bill*] bill of exchange, a written order from one person to another to
pay a certain sum to a third person; a kind of check.
47. *engrossed*] monopolized.

BONIFACE.
> Who shall I tell him, sir, would—

AIMWELL.
> Ha, that stroke was well thrown in. —I'm only a traveler   60
> like himself and would be glad of his company, that's all.

BONIFACE.
> I obey your commands, as the saying is.   *Exit.*

> *Enter* Archer.

ARCHER.
> S'death, I had forgot! What title will you give yourself?

AIMWELL.
> My brother's, to be sure. He would never give me any-
> thing else, so I'll make bold with his honor this bout.   65
> You know the rest of your cue.

ARCHER.
> Ay, ay.   *Exit.*

> *Enter* Gibbet.

GIBBET.
> Sir, I'm yours.

AIMWELL.
> 'Tis more than I deserve, sir, for I don't know you.

GIBBET.
> I don't wonder at that, sir, for you never saw me before,   70
> (*aside*) I hope.

AIMWELL.
> And pray, sir, how came I by the honor of seeing you
> now?

GIBBET.
> Sir, I scorn to intrude upon any gentleman, but my land-
> lord—   75

AIMWELL.
> O, sir, I ask your pardon. You're the captain he told me
> of.

GIBBET.
> At your service, sir.

AIMWELL.
> What regiment, may I be so bold?

67. S.D. *Exit*] Q2; *Exit* Boniface *Q1*.

GIBBET.

A marching regiment, sir, an old corps.   80

AIMWELL (aside).

Very old, if your coat be regimental. —You have served
abroad, sir?

GIBBET.

Yes, sir, in the plantations; 'twas my lot to be sent into
the worst service. I would have quitted it indeed, but a
man of honor, you know—besides 'twas for the good of   85
my country that I should be abroad. Anything for the
good of one's country. I'm a Roman for that.

AIMWELL (aside).

One of the first, I'll lay my life. —You found the West
Indies very hot, sir?

GIBBET.

Ay, sir, too hot for me.   90

AIMWELL.

Pray, sir, han't I seen your face at Will's Coffeehouse?

GIBBET.

Yes, sir, and at White's too.

AIMWELL.

And where is your company now, captain?

GIBBET.

They an't come yet.

AIMWELL.

Why, d'ye expect 'em here?   95

GIBBET.

They'll be here tonight, sir.

AIMWELL.

Which way do they march?

---

83. *the plantations*] the colonies. Felons were frequently transported to
the plantations.

87. *Roman*] a foot soldier who gave up his pay to his captain for permis-
sion to work, thereby "serving, like an ancient Roman, for glory, and the
love of his country" (*OED*).

91. *Will's Coffeehouse*] a coffeehouse at No. 1 Bow Street, Covent Garden, patronized by literary men. It was named after its original propri-
etor, William Urwin.

92. *White's*] a chocolate-house at Nos. 37 and 38 St. James's Street, established ca. 1698 by Francis White. Early in the eighteenth century it had
become a gaming house for the aristocracy. It became a club in 1736.

GIBBET.

Across the country. —[*Aside*.] The devil's in't, if I han't
said enough to encourage him to declare, but I'm afraid
he's not right. I must tack about.   100

AIMWELL.

Is your company to quarter in Lichfield?

GIBBET.

In this house, sir.

AIMWELL.

What, all?

GIBBET.

My company's but thin, ha, ha, ha; we are but three, ha,
ha, ha.   105

AIMWELL.

You're merry, sir.

GIBBET.

Ay, sir, you must excuse me, sir. I understand the world,
especially the art of traveling. I don't care, sir, for an-
swering questions directly upon the road, for I generally
ride with a charge about me.   110

AIMWELL (*aside*).

Three or four, I believe.

GIBBET.

I am credibly informed that there are highwaymen
upon this quarter; not, sir, that I could suspect a gentleman of your figure. But truly, sir, I have got such a
way of evasion upon the road that I don't care for speak- 115
ing truth to any man.

AIMWELL.

Your caution may be necessary. Then I presume you're
no captain?

GIBBET.

Not I, sir. Captain is a good traveling name, and so I
take it. It stops a great many foolish inquiries that are 120
generally made about gentlemen that travel. It gives a
man an air of something and makes the drawers obe-

---

100. *tack about*] change direction; a naval term.
110. *charge*] a sum of money, a quantity of gunpowder, an accusation of
a crime. Gibbet clearly intends the first, Aimwell, the second and third.
122. *drawers*] drawers of liquor, waiters in taprooms.

dient. And thus far I am a captain and no farther.

AIMWELL.

And pray, sir, what is your true profession?

GIBBET.

O, sir, you must excuse me. Upon my word, sir, I don't 125
think it safe to tell you.

AIMWELL.

Ha, ha, ha, upon my word I commend you.

Enter Boniface.

Well, Mr. Boniface, what's the news?

BONIFACE.

There's another gentleman below, as the saying is, that
hearing you were but two would be glad to make the 130
third man if you would give him leave.

AIMWELL.

What is he?

BONIFACE.

A clergyman, as the saying is.

AIMWELL.

A clergyman! Is he really a clergyman, or is it only his
traveling name, as my friend the captain has it? 135

BONIFACE.

O, sir, he's a priest and chaplain to the French officers in
town.

AIMWELL.

Is he a Frenchman?

BONIFACE.

Yes, sir, born at Brussels.

GIBBET.

A Frenchman, and a priest! I won't be seen in his com- 140
pany, sir. I have a value for my reputation, sir.

AIMWELL.

Nay, but captain, since we are by ourselves— Can he
speak English, landlord?

BONIFACE.

Very well, sir. You may know him, as the saying is, to be
a foreigner by his accent, and that's all. 145

AIMWELL.

Then he has been in England before?

BONIFACE.

Never, sir, but he's a master of languages, as the saying
is. He talks Latin. It does me good to hear him talk
Latin.

AIMWELL.

Then you understand Latin, Mr. Boniface?   150

BONIFACE.

Not I, sir, as the saying is, but he talks it so very fast that
I'm sure it must be good.

AIMWELL.

Pray desire him to walk up.

BONIFACE.

Here he is, as the saying is.

Enter Foigard.

FOIGARD.

Save you, gentlemens, both.   155

AIMWELL [*aside*].

A Frenchman! —Sir, your most humble servant.

FOIGARD.

Och, dear joy, I am your most faithful shervant, and
yours alsho.

GIBBET.

Doctor, you talk very good English, but you have a
mighty twang of the foreigner.   160

FOIGARD.

My English is very vel for the vords, but we foregners,
you know, cannot bring our tongues about the pronun-
ciation so soon.

AIMWELL (*aside*).

A foreigner! A downright Teague by this light. —Were
you born in France, doctor?   165

FOIGARD.

I was educated in France, but I was borned at Brussels. I
am a subject of the King of Spain, joy.

---

157. *joy*] a term of endearment traditionally associated with Irish
speech.

164. *Teague*] a nickname for an Irishman.

GIBBET.

> What King of Spain, sir? Speak.

FOIGARD.

> Upon my shoul, joy, I cannot tell you as yet.

AIMWELL.

> Nay, captain, that was too hard upon the doctor. He's a   170
> stranger.

FOIGARD.

> O, let him alone, dear joy. I am of a nation that is not
> easily put out of countenance.

AIMWELL.

> Come, gentlemen, I'll end the dispute. —Here, land-
> lord, is dinner ready?   175

BONIFACE.

> Upon the table, as the saying is.

AIMWELL.

> Gentlemen—pray—that door—

FOIGARD.

> No, no, fait, the captain must lead.

AIMWELL.

> No, doctor, the church is our guide.

GIBBET.

> Ay, ay, so it is.   *Exit foremost; they follow.* 180

[III.iii]

> *Scene changes to a gallery in Lady Bountiful's house.*
> *Enter* Archer *and* Scrub *singing, and hugging one another,* Scrub *with*
> *a tankard in his hand,* Gipsy *listening at a distance.*

SCRUB.

> Tall, all dall. Come, my dear boy, let's have that song
> once more.

ARCHER.

> No, no, we shall disturb the family. But will you be sure
> to keep the secret?

SCRUB.

> Pho, upon my honor, as I'm a gentleman.   5

---

168. *What King of Spain*] The War of the Spanish Succession was fought
at least in part to decide whether Philip, the grandson of Louis XIV, or
the Archduke Charles of Austria (later Holy Roman Emperor) would be
King of Spain. The former, as Philip V, ultimately prevailed.

ARCHER.

'Tis enough. You must know then that my master is the
Lord Viscount Aimwell. He fought a duel t'other day in
London, wounded his man so dangerously that he
thinks fit to withdraw till he hears whether the gentleman's wounds be mortal or not. He never was in this   10
part of England before, so he chose to retire to this
place; that's all.

GIPSY.

And that's enough for me.   *Exit.*

SCRUB.

And where were you when your master fought?

ARCHER.

We never know of our masters' quarrels.   15

SCRUB.

No, if our masters in the country here receive a challenge, the first thing they do is to tell their wives, the
wife tells the servants, the servants alarm the tenants,
and in half an hour you shall have the whole county in
arms.   20

ARCHER.

To hinder two men from doing what they have no mind
for. But if you should chance to talk now of my business?

SCRUB.

Talk! Ay, sir, had I not learnt the knack of holding my
tongue, I had never lived so long in a great family.   25

ARCHER.

Ay, ay, to be sure, there are secrets in all families.

SCRUB.

Secrets, ay, but I'll say no more. Come, sit down. We'll
make an end of our tankard. Here—

ARCHER.

With all my heart. Who knows but you and I may come
to be better acquainted, eh? Here's your ladies' healths.   30
You have three, I think, and to be sure there must be
secrets among 'em.

SCRUB.

Secrets! Ay, friend. I wish I had a friend.

ARCHER.

Am not I your friend? Come, you and I will be sworn
brothers.   35

SCRUB.

Shall we?

ARCHER.

From this minute. Give me a kiss. And now, Brother
Scrub—

SCRUB.

And now, Brother Martin, I will tell you a secret that will
make your hair stand on end. You must know that I am   40
consumedly in love.

ARCHER.

That's a terrible secret, that's the truth on't.

SCRUB.

That jade, Gipsy, that was with us just now in the cellar,
is the arrantest whore that ever wore a petticoat, and I'm
dying for love of her.   45

ARCHER.

Ha, ha, ha. Are you in love with her person or her
virtue, Brother Scrub?

SCRUB.

I should like virtue best because it is more durable than
beauty; for virtue holds good with some women long,
and many a day after they have lost it.   50

ARCHER.

In the country, I grant ye, where no woman's virtue is
lost till a bastard be found.

SCRUB.

Ay, could I bring her to a bastard I should have her all
to myself, but I dare not put it upon that lay for fear of
being sent for a soldier. Pray, brother, how do you gen-   55
tlemen in London like that same Pressing Act?

---

54. *put . . . lay*] take that line of action.

56. *Pressing Act*] From 1703 on, because of the difficulty in recruiting
men for the war, annual acts were passed empowering justices of the
peace to levy as recruits all able-bodied men who had no visible employ-
ment or means of subsistence. Also subject to impressment were debtors
and other offenders, who were discharged from prison on condition of
enlistment.

ARCHER.

Very ill, Brother Scrub. 'Tis the worst that ever was
made for us. Formerly I remember the good days when
we could dun our masters for our wages, and if they
refused to pay us we could have a warrant to carry 'em   60
before a justice. But now if we talk of eating they have a
warrant for us and carry us before three justices.

SCRUB.

And to be sure we go if we talk of eating, for the justices
won't give their own servants a bad example. Now this is
my misfortune: I dare not speak in the house while that   65
jade Gipsy dings about like a fury. Once I had the better
end of the staff.

ARCHER.

And how comes the change now?

SCRUB.

Why, the mother of all this mischief is a priest.

ARCHER.

A priest!   70

SCRUB.

Ay, a damned son of a Whore of Babylon, that came
over hither to say grace to the French officers and eat up
our provisions. There's not a day goes over his head
without dinner or supper in this house.

ARCHER.

How came he so familiar in the family?   75

SCRUB.

Because he speaks English as if he had lived here all his
life and tells lies as if he had been a traveler from his
cradle.

ARCHER.

And this priest, I'm afraid, has converted the affections
of your Gipsy.   80

SCRUB.

Converted, ay, and perverted, my dear friend, for I'm
afraid he has made her a whore and a papist. But this is

---

66. *dings*] flings, bounces.

66–67. *better . . . staff*] advantage. Cf. contemporary "short end of the
stick," meaning "disadvantage."

71. *Whore of Babylon*] the Church of Rome; an allusion to Revelation 17.

not all. There's the French count and Mrs. Sullen;
they're in the confederacy, and for some private ends
of their own, to be sure.   85

ARCHER.

A very hopeful family yours, Brother Scrub. I suppose
the maiden lady has her lover too.

SCRUB.

Not that I know. She's the best on 'em, that's the truth
on't. But they take care to prevent my curiosity by giving
me so much business that I'm a perfect slave. What d'ye   90
think is my place in this family?

ARCHER.

Butler, I suppose.

SCRUB.

Ah, Lord help you. I'll tell you. Of a Monday, I drive the
coach. Of a Tuesday, I drive the plough. On Wednesday, I follow the hounds. A-Thursday, I dun the ten-   95
ants. On Friday, I go to market. On Saturday, I draw
warrants. And a-Sunday, I draw beer.

ARCHER.

Ha, ha, ha! If variety be a pleasure in life you have
enough on't, my dear brother. But what ladies are
those?   100

SCRUB.

Ours, ours. That upon the right hand is Mrs. Sullen,
and the other is Mrs. Dorinda. Don't mind 'em. Sit still,
man.

Enter Mrs. Sullen, *and* Dorinda.

MRS. SULLEN.

I have heard my brother talk of my Lord Aimwell, but
they say that his brother is the finer gentleman.   105

DORINDA.

That's impossible, sister.

MRS. SULLEN.

He's vastly rich, but very close, they say.

101. S.P. SCRUB] *O;* ARCHER *Q1.*

96–97. *draw warrants*] write out authorizations of payment (or orders for
delivery of goods), probably to tradesmen.

DORINDA.

No matter for that. If I can creep into his heart I'll open
his breast, I warrant him. I have heard say that people
may be guessed at by the behavior of their servants. I 110
could wish we might talk to that fellow.

MRS. SULLEN.

So do I, for I think he's a very pretty fellow. Come this
way. I'll throw out a lure for him presently.

They walk a turn towards the opposite side of the stage.

ARCHER [*aside*].

Corn, wine, and oil, indeed! But, I think, the wife has
the greatest plenty of flesh and blood; she should be my 115
choice.   Mrs. Sullen *drops her glove.*
Aha, say you so—

Archer *runs, takes it up, and gives it to her.*

Madam, your ladyship's glove.

MRS. SULLEN.

O, sir, I thank you. —[*To* Dorinda.]   What a handsome
bow that fellow has!   120

DORINDA.

Bow! Why I have known several footmen come down
from London set up here for dancing-masters and carry
off the best fortunes in the country.

ARCHER (*aside*).

That project, for ought I know, had been better than
ours. —Brother Scrub, why don't you introduce me?   125

SCRUB.

Ladies, this is the strange gentleman's servant that you
see at church today. I understood he came from London, and so I invited him to the cellar that he might
show me the newest flourish in whetting my knives.

DORINDA.

And I hope you have made much of him?   130

ARCHER.

O, yes, madam, but the strength of your ladyship's

---

116. S.D. *glove*] *Q1; fan W6.*   118. glove] *Q1;* fan *W6.*
117. Aha,] Ah, a, *Q1.*   120. has] *Q1;* made *D2.*

liquor is a little too potent for the constitution of your
humble servant.

MRS. SULLEN.

What, then you don't usually drink ale?

ARCHER.

No, madam, my constant drink is tea or a little wine and 135
water. 'Tis prescribed me by the physician for a remedy
against the spleen.

SCRUB.

O la, O la! A footman have the spleen!

MRS. SULLEN.

I thought that distemper had been only proper to
people of quality.   140

ARCHER.

Madam, like all other fashions it wears out and so de-
scends to their servants, though in a great many of us, I
believe, it proceeds from some melancholy particles in
the blood occasioned by the stagnation of wages.

DORINDA [aside].

How affectedly the fellow talks. —How long, pray, have 145
you served your present master?

ARCHER.

Not long. My life has been mostly spent in the service of
the ladies.

MRS. SULLEN.

And pray, which service do you like best?

ARCHER.

Madam, the ladies pay best. The honor of serving them 150
is sufficient wages; there is a charm in their looks that
delivers a pleasure with their commands and gives our
duty the wings of inclination.

MRS. SULLEN [to Dorinda].

That flight was above the pitch of a livery. —[To
Archer.] And, sir, would not you be satisfied to serve a 155
lady again?

ARCHER.

As a groom of the chamber, madam, but not as a footman.

136. physician] Q1; physicians Q2.

_____

137. *spleen*] depression, irritability.

MRS. SULLEN.

I suppose you served as footman before.

ARCHER.

For that reason I would not serve in that post again, for   160
my memory is too weak for the load of messages that the
ladies lay upon their servants in London. My Lady
Howd'ye, the last mistress I served, called me up one
morning and told me, "Martin, go to my Lady Allnight
with my humble service. Tell her I was to wait on her   165
ladyship yesterday and left word with Mrs. Rebecca that
the preliminaries of the affair she knows of are stopped
till we know the concurrence of the person that I know
of, for which there are circumstances wanting which we
shall accommodate at the old place; but that in the   170
meantime there is a person about her ladyship, that
from several hints and surmises, was accessary at a certain time to the disappointments that naturally attend
things that to her knowledge are of more importance."

MRS. SULLEN. DORINDA.

Ha, ha, ha! Where are you going, sir?   175

ARCHER.

Why, I han't half done. The whole howd'ye was about
half an hour long, so I happened to misplace two sylla-
bles and was turned off and rendered incapable.

DORINDA.

The pleasantest fellow, sister, I ever saw. —But, friend,
if your master be married, I presume you still serve a   180
lady.

ARCHER.

No, madam, I take care never to come into a married
family; the commands of the master and mistress are
always so contrary that 'tis impossible to please both.

DORINDA (aside).

There's a main point gained. My lord is not married, I   185
find.

MRS. SULLEN.

But, I wonder, friend, that in so many good services you
had not a better provision made for you.

---

178. *turned off*] discharged, dismissed.

ARCHER.

I don't know how, madam. I had a lieutenancy offered
me three or four times, but that is not bread, madam. I   190
live much better as I do.

SCRUB.

Madam, he sings rarely. I was thought to do pretty well
here in the country till he came, but alack-a-day, I'm
nothing to my brother Martin.

DORINDA.

Does he? Pray, sir, will you oblige us with a song?   195

ARCHER.

Are you for passion or humor?

SCRUB.

O la, he has the purest ballad about a trifle.

MRS. SULLEN.

A trifle! Pray, sir, let's have it.

ARCHER.

I'm ashamed to offer you a trifle, madam, but since you
command me—   200

Sings to the tune of Sir Simon the King.

A trifling song you shall hear,
Begun with a trifle and ended.
All trifling people draw near,
And I shall be nobly attended.

Were it not for trifles, a few   205

197. la] *W6;* le *Q1.*   *full, after the Epilogue); Q1–2 and*
210–52. A trifling ... to boot]*W6*   *many other 18th-century eds. print only*
(which is the first ed. to print the song in   *first two lines at this point.*

200.1. *Sir Simon the King*] A popular ballad, known also as "Old Simon
the King" and reputedly named for Simon Wardloe, the owner of the
Devil Tavern patronized by Ben Jonson. The traditional tune is printed,
among other places, in Henry Playford's *The Dancing Master,* supplement
to the 6th edition, 1679. In the eighteenth century, a number of broadside
ballads were sung to the tune, and seven ballad operas, including John
Gay's *The Beggar's Opera* (1728), made use of it. For a history of the tune
and the ballads sung to it, see Claude M. Simpson, *The British Broadside
Ballad and Its Music* (New Brunswick, N. J., 1966), pp. 545–51. It is possible that at least in some performances of *The Beaux' Stratagem* "The Trifle"
was sung to a tune composed by Daniel Purcell (ca. 1660–1717), published
in broadsheets, probably in 1707, as *"The Trifle:* A New Song Set by Mr. D.
Purcell" (copies in the British Museum and the Huntington Library).

That lately have come into play,
The men would want something to do,
And the women want something to say.

What makes men trifle in dressing?
Because the ladies (they know)   210
Admire, by often possessing,
That eminent trifle, a beau.

When the lover his moments has trifled
The trifle of trifles to gain,
No sooner the virgin is rifled,   215
But a trifle shall part 'em again.

What mortal man would be able
At White's half an hour to sit?
Or who could bear a tea table
Without talking of trifles for wit?   220

The court is from trifles secure;
Gold keys are no trifles, we see;
White rods are no trifles, I'm sure,
Whatever their bearers may be.

But if you will go to the place   225
Where trifles abundantly breed,
The levee will show you his grace
Makes promises trifles indeed.

A coach with six footmen behind
I count neither trifle nor sin,   230
But, ye gods, how oft do we find
A scandalous trifle within?

A flask of champagne, people think it
A trifle, or something as bad;

---

218. *White's*] a chocolate-house; see note for III.ii.92.

222. *Gold keys*] symbols of office of the groom of the stole and other court positions.

223. *White rods*] symbols of office of the Lord Treasurer, the Lord Steward, the Lord Chamberlain (who was, among other duties, responsible for regulating the theater), and the Earl Marshal.

227. *levee*] a reception held by members of the royal family or of the nobility on rising from bed.

227. *his grace*] reputed to be an allusion to the Duke of Ormond's failure to keep a promise to Farquhar.

But if you'll contrive how to drink it   235
You'll find it no trifle, egad.

A parson's a trifle at sea,
A widow's a trifle in sorrow,
A peace is a trifle today,
Who knows what may happen tomorrow?   240

A black coat a trifle may cloak,
Or to hide it the red may endeavor;
But if once the army is broke,
We shall have more trifles than ever.

The stage is a trifle, they say;   245
The reason pray carry along,
Because at every new play
The house they with trifles so throng.

But with people's malice to trifle
And to set us all on a foot   250
The author of this is a trifle,
And his song is a trifle to boot.

MRS. SULLEN.

Very well, sir, we're obliged to you. Something for a pair
of gloves.   *Offering him money.*

ARCHER.

I humbly beg leave to be excused. My master, 255
madam, pays me, nor dare I take money from any other
hand without injuring his honor and disobeying his
commands.   *Exit.*

DORINDA.

This is surprising. Did you ever see so pretty a well-bred
fellow?   260

MRS. SULLEN.

The devil take him for wearing that livery.

DORINDA.

I fancy, sister, he may be some gentleman, a friend of

---

239. *peace*] no doubt an allusion to the Tories' efforts to bring about a
peace with France.
241. *black coat*] that of the clergyman.
242. *the red*] the red coat of the soldier.
243. *broke*] disbanded, dissolved.

my lord's, that his lordship has pitched upon for his
courage, fidelity, and discretion to bear him company in
this dress, and who, ten to one, was his second too.   265

MRS. SULLEN.

It is so, it must be so, and it shall be so. For I like him.

DORINDA.

What, better than the count?

MRS. SULLEN.

The count happened to be the most agreeable man
upon the place, and so I chose him to serve me in my
design upon my husband. But I should like this fellow 270
better in a design upon myself.

DORINDA.

But now, sister, for an interview with this lord and this
gentleman; how shall we bring that about?

MRS. SULLEN.

Patience! You country ladies give no quarter if once you
be entered. Would you prevent their desires and give 275
the fellows no wishing time? Look ye, Dorinda, if my
Lord Aimwell loves you or deserves you he'll find a way
to see you, and there we must leave it. My business
comes now upon the tapis. Have you prepared your
brother?   280

DORINDA.

Yes, yes.

MRS. SULLEN.

And how did he relish it?

DORINDA.

He said little, mumbled something to himself, promised
to be guided by me. But here he comes.

Enter Sullen.

SULLEN.

What singing was that I heard just now?   285

---

275. *be entered*] entered upon a course of action or conduct. Like many
of Mrs. Sullen's comments, however, this one has sexual connotations.

275. *prevent*] anticipate; "to act as if the event or time had already come"
(*OED*).

279. *upon the tapis*] under consideration or discussion (literally "on the
tablecloth").

MRS. SULLEN.

The singing in your head, my dear. You complained of
it all day.

SULLEN.

You're impertinent.

MRS. SULLEN.

I was ever so since I became one flesh with you.

SULLEN.

One flesh! Rather two carcasses joined unnaturally to-   290
gether.

MRS. SULLEN.

Or rather a living soul coupled to a dead body.

DORINDA.

So, this is fine encouragement for me.

SULLEN.

Yes, my wife shows you what you must do.

MRS. SULLEN.

And my husband shows you what you must suffer.   295

SULLEN.

S'death, why can't you be silent?

MRS. SULLEN.

S'death, why can't you talk?

SULLEN.

Do you talk to any purpose?

MRS. SULLEN.

Do you think to any purpose?

SULLEN.

Sister, hark ye. *(Whispers.)* —I shan't be home till it be   300
late.   *Exit.*

MRS. SULLEN.

What did he whisper to ye?

286. your] *Q2;* you're *Q1.*

290–92. *One flesh . . . body*] In his "The Influence of Milton's Divorce
Tracts on Farquhar's *Beaux' Stratagem*," *PMLA* 39 (1924): 174–78, Martin
A. Larson points out that these lines seem to be "lifted whole" from
Doctrine and Discipline of Divorce: "nay instead of beeing one flesh, they will
be rather two carkasses chain'd unnaturally together; or as it may happ'n,
a living soule bound to a dead corps" (*Complete Prose Works of John Milton*
[New Haven, Connecticut, 1959], 2:326). Unless otherwise indicated, Mil-
ton quotations are from *Doctrine and Discipline.*

DORINDA.

That he would go round the back way, come into the
closet, and listen as I directed him. But let me beg you
once more, dear sister, to drop this project, for, as I told   305
you before, instead of awaking him to kindness you may
provoke him to a rage. And then who knows how far his
brutality may carry him?

MRS. SULLEN.

I'm provided to receive him, I warrant you. But here
comes the count. Vanish.   *Exit* Dorinda.   310

                    Enter Count Bellair.

Don't you wonder, Monsieur le Count, that I was not at
church this afternoon?

COUNT.

I more wonder, madam, that you go dere at all or how
you dare to lift those eyes to heaven that are guilty of so
much killing.   315

MRS. SULLEN.

If heaven, sir, has given to my eyes, with the power of
killing, the virtue of making a cure, I hope the one may
atone for the other.

COUNT.

O largely, madam. Would your ladyship be as ready to
apply the remedy as to give the wound? Consider,   320
madam, I am doubly a prisoner: first to the arms of your
general, then to your more conquering eyes. My first
chains are easy—there a ransom may redeem me—but
from your fetters I never shall get free.

MRS. SULLEN.

Alas, sir, why should you complain to me of your captiv-   325
ity, who am in chains myself? You know, sir, that I am
bound, nay, must be tied up in that particular that might
give you ease: I am like you a prisoner of war—of war
indeed. I have given my parole of honor. Would you
break yours to gain your liberty?   330

---

327. must] *Q2;* most *Q1.*

329. *parole of honor*] word of honor; the promise made by a prisoner of
war not to escape.

COUNT.

Most certainly I would were I a prisoner among the
Turks. Dis is your case; you're a slave, madam, slave to
the worst of Turks, a husband.

MRS. SULLEN.

There lies my foible, I confess. No fortifications, no
courage, conduct, nor vigilancy can pretend to defend a 335
place where the cruelty of the governor forces the garri-
son to mutiny.

COUNT.

And where de besieger is resolved to die before de
place. Here will I fix; (*kneels*) with tears, vows, and
prayers assault your heart, and never rise till you sur- 340
render; or if I must storm—love and St. Michael. And so
I begin the attack.

MRS. SULLEN.

Stand off!—(*Aside.*) Sure he hears me not, and I could
almost wish he—did not. The fellow makes love very
prettily. —But, sir, why should you put such a value 345
upon my person when you see it despised by one that
knows it so much better?

COUNT.

He knows it not though he possesses it. If he but knew
the value of the jewel he is master of he would always
wear it next his heart and sleep with it in his arms.   350

MRS. SULLEN.

But since he throws me unregarded from him—

COUNT.

And one that knows your value well comes by and takes
you up, is it not justice?   *Goes to lay hold on her.*

Enter Sullen *with his sword drawn.*

SULLEN.

Hold, villain, hold.

MRS. SULLEN (*presenting a pistol*).

Do you hold.   355

---

341. *St. Michael*] This saint, who headed the armies of heaven, was
venerated as the patron of soldiers.

SULLEN.

What, murther your husband to defend your bully?

MRS. SULLEN.

Bully! For shame, Mr. Sullen. Bullies wear long swords.
The gentleman has none; he's a prisoner, you know. I
was aware of your outrage and prepared this to receive
your violence, and, if occasion were, to preserve myself 360
against the force of this other gentleman.

COUNT.

O, madam, your eyes be bettre firearms than your pistol; they nevre miss.

SULLEN.

What, court my wife to my face!

MRS. SULLEN.

Pray, Mr. Sullen, put up; suspend your fury for a min- 365
ute.

SULLEN.

To give you time to invent an excuse.

MRS. SULLEN.

I need none.

SULLEN.

No, for I heard every syllable of your discourse.

COUNT.

Ay, and begar, I tink de dialogue was vera pretty.   370

MRS. SULLEN.

Then I suppose, sir, you heard something of your own
barbarity.

SULLEN.

Barbarity! Oons, what does the woman call barbarity?
Do I ever meddle with you?

MRS. SULLEN.

No.   375

SULLEN.

As for you, sir, I shall take another time.

COUNT.

Ah, begar, and so must I.

---

356. *bully*] protector of a prostitute; one who lives by protecting prosti-
tutes. *OED* cites this passage.
370. *begar*] by God. Cf. begad.

SULLEN.

Look'ee, madam, don't think that my anger proceeds
from any concern I have for your honor, but for my
own, and if you can contrive any way of being a whore   380
without making me a cuckold, do it and welcome.

MRS. SULLEN.

Sir, I thank you kindly. You would allow me the sin but
rob me of the pleasure. No, no, I'm resolved never to
venture upon the crime without the satisfaction of seeing you punished for't.   385

SULLEN.

Then will you grant me this, my dear? Let anybody else
do you the favor but that Frenchman, for I mortally
hate his whole generation.   *Exit.*

COUNT.

Ah, sir, that be ungrateful, for begar, I love some of
yours, madam.   *Approaching her.* 390

MRS. SULLEN.

No, sir.

COUNT.

No, sir! Garzoon, madam, I am not your husband.

MRS. SULLEN.

'Tis time to undeceive you, sir. I believed your addresses
to me were no more than an amusement, and I hope
you will think the same of my complaisance. And to   395
convince you that you ought, you must know that I
brought you hither only to make you instrumental in
setting me right with my husband, for he was planted to
listen by my appointment.

COUNT.

By your appointment?   400

MRS. SULLEN.

Certainly.

COUNT.

And so, madam, while I was telling twenty stories to part

---

387. *the favor*] a euphemism for sexual favors; also referred to as "the
last favor."

388. *generation*] "family, breed, race; class, kind, or 'set' of persons"
(*OED*).

392. *Garzoon*] God's wounds.

you from your husband, begar, I was bringing you together all the while.

MRS. SULLEN.

I ask your pardon, sir, but I hope this will give you a   405
taste of the virtue of the English ladies.

COUNT.

Begar, madam, your virtue be vera great, but garzoon,
your honeste be vera little.

Enter Dorinda.

MRS. SULLEN.

Nay, now you're angry, sir.

COUNT.

Angry! Fair Dorinda.   410

Sings Dorinda *the opera tune and addresses to* Dorinda.

Madam, when your ladyship want a fool, send for me.
"Fair Dorinda, Revenge, etc."   *Exit.*

MRS. SULLEN.

There goes the true humor of his nation: resentment
with good manners and the height of anger in a song.
Well sister, you must be judge, for you have heard the   415
trial.

DORINDA.

And I bring in my brother guilty.

MRS. SULLEN.

But I must bear the punishment. 'Tis hard, sister.

DORINDA.

I own it, but you must have patience.

407. be] *C;* de *Q1.*

---

410. *Fair Dorinda*] most likely, as Stonehill surmises (2: 440), the song
sung by the Baroness as Lavinia in Act I, scene ix, of the opera *Camilla,*
with music by Marc Antonio Bononcini and a libretto, translated from the
Italian (*Il Trionfo di Camilla,* 1697) of Silvio Stampiglia, by Owen
MacSwiney: "Fair Dorinda, happy, happy/ Happy may'st thou ever be." In
Act II, scene i, Camilla (alias Dorinda throughout the opera) ends a
speech with these lines, evidently sung: "Revenge! Revenge! I summon!/
Revenge is all my Care;/ Revenge! I summon; yet no." It is possible that the
Count sings or hums bits of both songs. Farquhar attacked the opera in
the Epilogue to *The Recruiting Officer.* It is interesting to note that
Katherine Tofts (see explanatory note to III.ii.38 above) sang the role of
Camilla/Dorinda.

MRS. SULLEN.

Patience, the cant of custom! Providence sends no evil   420
without a remedy. Should I lie groaning under a yoke I
can shake off I were accessary to my ruin, and my patience were no better than self-murder.

DORINDA.

But how can you shake off the yoke? Your divisions
don't come within the reach of the law for a divorce.   425

MRS. SULLEN.

Law! What law can search into the remote abyss of
nature? What evidence can prove the unaccountable
disaffections of wedlock? Can a jury sum up the endless
aversions that are rooted in our souls, or can a bench
give judgment upon antipathies?   430

DORINDA.

They never pretend it, sister. They never meddle but in
case of uncleanness.

MRS. SULLEN.

Uncleanness! O, sister, casual violation is a transient in-
jury and may possibly be repaired, but can radical ha-
treds be ever reconciled? No, no, sister, nature is the   435
first lawgiver, and when she has set tempers opposite,
not all the golden links of wedlock nor iron manacles of
law can keep 'um fast.

431. pretend it] *Q2;* pretended *Q1.*

421–23. *Should . . . self-murder*] Milton (as Larson points out, though
citing no specific passages) suggests that suffering under the yoke of an
ill-mated marriage is a form of self-destruction. A man, at any rate, should
be able to "break the error of his own bonds with an unfit and mistak'n
wife, to the saving of his welfare, his life, yea his faith and vertue from the
hazard of overstrong temptations" (*Prose Works*, 2:274). In *Tetrachordon,*
Milton asks, "Can any law or command be so unreasonable as to make
men cleav to calamity, to ruin, to perdition?" (ibid., p. 605).
426–30. *What law . . . antipathies?*] "The causes of seeking divorce," Milton writes, "reside so deeply in the radical and innocent affections of
nature, as is not within the diocese of Law to tamper with" (ibid., p. 345).
He further comments that Christ did not authorize "a judiciall Court to
tosse about and divulge the unaccountable and secret reasons of disaffec-
tion between man & wife," that these reasons are "most improperly an-
swerable to any such kind of trial" (ibid., p. 343).
434. *radical*] inherent,. fundamental.
433–38. *casual . . . fast*] Two statements of Milton's are relevant here:
"natural hatred whenever it arises, is a greater evil in marriage, then the

Wedlock we own ordained by heaven's decree,
But such as heaven ordained it first to be: 440
Concurring tempers in the man and wife
As mutual helps to draw the load of life.
View all the works of Providence above;
The stars with harmony and concord move.
View all the works of Providence below;   445
The fire, the water, earth, and air we know
All in one plant agree to make it grow.
Must man, the chiefest work of art divine,
Be doomed in endless discord to repine?
No, we should injure heaven by that surmise;   450
Omnipotence is just, were man but wise.

End of the Third Act.

---

accident of adultery, a greater defrauding, a greater injustice, and yet not
blameable" (*Prose Works*, 2:332); and "To couple hatred therfore though
wedlock try all her golden links, and borrow to her aid all the iron manacles and fetters of Law, it does but seek to twist a rope of sand" (ibid., p.
345).

ACT IV

Scene continues.
                              Enter Mrs. Sullen.

MRS. SULLEN.

Were I born an humble Turk, where women have no
soul nor property, there I must sit contented. But in
England, a country whose women are its glory, must
women be abused? Where women rule, must women be
enslaved, nay, cheated into slavery, mocked by a prom-   5
ise of comfortable society into a wilderness of solitude? I
dare not keep the thought about me. O, here comes
something to divert me.

Enter a Countrywoman.

WOMAN.

I come, an't please your ladyship. You're my Lady
Bountiful, an't ye?   10

MRS. SULLEN.

Well, good woman, go on.

WOMAN.

I come seventeen long mail to have a cure for my husband's sore leg.

MRS. SULLEN.

Your husband! What, woman, cure your husband?

WOMAN.

Ay, poor man, for his sore leg won't let him stir from   15
home.

MRS. SULLEN.

There, I confess, you have given me a reason. Well,
good woman, I'll tell you what you must do. You must
lay your husband's leg upon a table, and with a chop-
ping knife you must lay it open as broad as you can.   20
Then you must take out the bone and beat the flesh
soundly with a rolling pin. Then take salt, pepper,

9. ladyship] *Q2;* ladyships *Q1.*

-74-

cloves, mace and ginger, some sweet herbs, and season it
very well. Then roll it up like brawn and put it into the
oven for two hours.   25

WOMAN.

Heavens reward your ladyship. I have two little babies
too that are piteous bad with the graips, an't please ye.

MRS. SULLEN.

Put a little pepper and salt in their bellies, good woman.

Enter Lady Bountiful.

I beg your ladyship's pardon for taking your business
out of your hands. I have been a-tampering here a little   30
with one of your patients.

LADY BOUNTIFUL.

Come, good woman, don't mind this mad creature. I am
the person that you want, I suppose. What would you
have, woman?

MRS. SULLEN.

She wants something for her husband's sore leg.   35

LADY BOUNTIFUL.

What's the matter with his leg, Goody?

WOMAN.

It come first, as one might say, with a sort of dizziness in
his foot, then he had a kind of a laziness in his joints, and
then his leg broke out, and then it swelled, and then it
closed again, and then it broke out again, and then it   40
festered, and then it grew better, and then it grew worse
again.

MRS. SULLEN.

Ha, ha, ha.

LADY BOUNTIFUL.

How can you be merry with the misfortunes of other
people?   45

MRS. SULLEN.

Because my own make me sad, madam.

---

24. *brawn*] "fleshy part, muscle, particularly the most fleshy part of the
hind leg, originally a part suitable for roasting" (*OED*). Sometimes used in
the specific sense of "boar's flesh."

27. *graips*] gripes, spasms.

36. *Goody*] a contraction of "good wife," a term applied to women in
humble life.

LADY BOUNTIFUL.

The worst reason in the world, daughter. Your own misfortunes should teach you to pity others.

MRS. SULLEN.

But the woman's misfortunes and mine are nothing alike. Her husband is sick, and mine, alas, is in health.　50

LADY BOUNTIFUL.

What, would you wish your husband sick?

MRS. SULLEN.

Not of a sore leg, of all things.

LADY BOUNTIFUL.

Well, good woman, go to the pantry; get your bellyful of victuals; then I'll give you a receipt of diet drink for your husband. But d'ye hear, Goody, you must not let your　55 husband move too much.

WOMAN.

No, no, madam, the poor man's inclinable enough to lie still.　　　　　　　　　　　　　　　　　　*Exit.*

LADY BOUNTIFUL.

Well, Daughter Sullen, though you laugh, I have done miracles about the country here with my receipts.　60

MRS. SULLEN.

Miracles indeed if they have cured anybody, but I believe, madam, the patient's faith goes farther toward the miracle than your prescription.

LADY BOUNTIFUL.

Fancy helps in some cases, but there's your husband, who has as little fancy as anybody. I brought him from　65 death's door.

MRS. SULLEN.

I suppose, madam, you made him drink plentifully of ass's milk.

Enter Dorinda, [*who*] *runs to* Mrs. Sullen.

DORINDA.

News, dear sister, news, news.

---

54. *receipt*] recipe; specifically, in this case, "remedy" or "means of cure."
68. *ass's milk*] frequently prescribed for persons in a weakened condition or with coughs.

Enter Archer *running.*

ARCHER.

Where, where is my Lady Bountiful? Pray, which is the   70
old lady of you three?

LADY BOUNTIFUL.

I am.

ARCHER.

O, madam, the fame of your ladyship's charity, goodness, benevolence, skill, and ability have drawn me
hither to implore your ladyship's help in behalf of my   75
unfortunate master, who is this moment breathing his
last.

LADY BOUNTIFUL.

Your master! Where is he?

ARCHER.

At your gate, madam. Drawn by the appearance of your
handsome house to view it nearer and walking up the   80
avenue within five paces of the courtyard, he was taken
ill of a sudden with a sort of I know not what, but down
he fell, and there he lies.

LADY BOUNTIFUL.

Here, Scrub, Gipsy, all run. Get my easy chair
downstairs, put the gentleman in it, and bring him in   85
quickly, quickly.

ARCHER.

Heaven will reward your ladyship for this charitable act.

LADY BOUNTIFUL.

Is your master used to these fits?

ARCHER.

O, yes, madam, frequently. I have known him have five
or six of a night.   90

LADY BOUNTIFUL.

What's his name?

ARCHER.

Lord, madam, he's a-dying. A minute's care or neglect
may save or destroy his life.

LADY BOUNTIFUL.

Ah, poor gentleman! Come, friend, show me the way.
I'll see him brought in myself.   95

Exit with Archer.

DORINDA.

O, sister, my heart flutters about strangely. I can hardly
forbear running to his assistance.

MRS. SULLEN.

And I'll lay my life he deserves your assistance more
then he wants it. Did not I tell you that my lord would
find a way to come at you? Love's his distemper, and you   100
must be the physician. Put on all your charms, summon
all your fire into your eyes, plant the whole artillery of
your looks against his breast, and down with him.

DORINDA.

O, sister, I'm but a young gunner. I shall be afraid to
shoot for fear the piece should recoil and hurt myself.   105

MRS. SULLEN.

Never fear; you shall see me shoot before you, if you
will.

DORINDA.

No, no, dear sister, you have missed your mark so un-
fortunately that I shan't care for being instructed by
you.   110

Enter Aimwell *in a chair, carried by* Archer *and* Scrub; Lady Bountiful, Gipsy. Aimwell *counterfeiting a swoon.*

LADY BOUNTIFUL.

Here, here, let's see the hartshorn drops. —Gipsy, a
glass of fair water. His fit's very strong. —Bless me, how
his hands are clinched.

ARCHER.

For shame, ladies, what d'ye do? Why don't you help us?
—(*To* Dorinda.)   Pray, madam, take his hand and open   115
it if you can whilst I hold his head.   Dorinda *takes his hand.*

DORINDA.

Poor gentleman. Oh! He has got my hand within his and
squeezes it unmercifully.

LADY BOUNTIFUL.

'Tis the violence of his convulsion, child.

---

99. *wants*] needs.
111. *hartshorn*] "the aqueous solution of ammonia (whether obtained
from harts' horns or otherwise)" (*OED*); a form of smelling salts.
112. *fair water*] clean or pure water.

ARCHER.

O, madam, he's perfectly possessed in these cases; he'll 120
bite if you don't have a care.

DORINDA.

Oh, my hand, my hand!

LADY BOUNTIFUL.

What's the matter with the foolish girl? I have got this
hand open, you see, with a great deal of ease.

ARCHER.

Ay, but, madam, your daughter's hand is somewhat 125
warmer than your ladyship's, and the heat of it draws
the force of the spirits that way.

MRS. SULLEN.

I find, friend, you're very learned in these sorts of fits.

ARCHER.

'Tis no wonder, madam, for I'm often troubled with
them myself. I find myself extremely ill at this minute. 130
Looking hard at Mrs. Sullen.

MRS. SULLEN (*aside*).

I fancy I could find a way to cure you.

LADY BOUNTIFUL.

His fit holds him very long.

ARCHER.

Longer than usual, madam. —Pray, young lady, open
his breast and give him air.

LADY BOUNTIFUL.

Where did his illness take him first, pray?   135

ARCHER.

Today at church, madam.

LADY BOUNTIFUL.

In what manner was he taken?

ARCHER.

Very strangely, my lady. He was of a sudden touched
with something in his eyes, which at the first he only felt
but could not tell whether 'twas pain or pleasure.   140

LADY BOUNTIFUL.

Wind, nothing but wind.

ARCHER.

By soft degrees it grew and mounted to his brain; there
his fancy caught it, there formed it so beautiful and

dressed it up in such gay pleasing colors that his transported appetite seized the fair idea and straight con-   145
veyed it to his heart. That hospitable seat of life sent all
its sanguine spirits forth to meet and opened all its sluicy
gates to take the stranger in.

LADY BOUNTIFUL.

Your master should never go without a bottle to smell
to. —Oh, he recovers, —The lavender water—some   150
feathers to burn under his nose—Hungary water to rub
his temples. —O, he comes to himself. —Hem a little,
sir, hem. —Gipsy, bring the cordial water.

                    Aimwell *seems to awake in amaze.*

DORINDA.

How d'ye, sir?

AIMWELL (*rising*).

Where am I?   155
    Sure I have passed the gulf of silent death,
    And now I land on the Elysian shore.
    Behold the goddess of those happy plains,
    Fair Proserpine. Let me adore thy bright divinity.

                    Kneels to Dorinda *and kisses her hand.*

MRS. SULLEN.

So, so, so, I knew where the fit would end.   160

AIMWELL.

    Eurydice perhaps—
        How could thy Orpheus keep his word
        And not look back upon thee?

---

151. *Hungary water*] a distilled water made from rosemary flowers. It
was supposed to relieve faintness.

153. *cordial water*] spirit, liquid produced by distillation.

157. *Elysian shore*] Elysium, known also as the Islands of the Blest, was in
Greek mythology the abode after death of those favored by the gods.

159. *Proserpine*] daughter of Jupiter and Ceres, carried off by Pluto to
be queen in the lower world. Through the intercession of Jupiter she was
allowed to live on earth for six (or eight) months of the year but required
to spend the rest of the year with Pluto in the lower world.

161–162. *Eurydice ... Orpheus*] The dryad Eurydice, wife of Orpheus,
died from a snake bite and went to the underworld. Orpheus went down
to Hades for her and by means of his music induced Proserpine to release
her, but only on the condition that Orpheus not look back at her as she
followed him. Shortly before emerging into the upper world, however,
Orpheus looked back at Eurydice, thereby losing her forever.

No treasure but thyself could sure have bribed him
To look one minute off thee.   165

LADY BOUNTIFUL.

Delirious, poor gentleman.

ARCHER.

Very delirious, madam, very delirious.

AIMWELL.

Martin's voice, I think.

ARCHER.

Yes, my lord. How does your lordship?

LADY BOUNTIFUL.

Lord! Did you mind that, girls?   170

AIMWELL.

Where am I?

ARCHER.

In very good hands, sir. You were taken just now with
one of your old fits under the trees just by this good
lady's house. Her ladyship had you taken in and has
miraculously brought you to yourself, as you see.   175

AIMWELL.

I am so confounded with shame, madam, that I can now
only beg pardon and refer my acknowledgments for
your ladyship's care till an opportunity offers of making
some amends. I dare be no longer troublesome. —Martin, give two guineas to the servants.   *Going.* 180

DORINDA.

Sir, you may catch cold by going so soon into the air.
You don't look, sir, as if you were perfectly recovered.

Here Archer *talks to* Lady Bountiful *in dumb show.*

AIMWELL.

That I shall never be, madam. My present illness is so
rooted that I must expect to carry it to my grave.

MRS. SULLEN.

Don't despair, sir; I have known several in your dis- 185
temper shake it off with a fortnight's physic.

LADY BOUNTIFUL.

Come, sir, your servant has been telling me that you're
apt to relapse if you go into the air. Your good manners
shan't get the better of ours. You shall sit down again,

sir; come, sir, we don't mind ceremonies in the country. 190
Here, sir, my service t'ye. You shall taste my water; 'tis a
cordial, I can assure you, and of my own making. Drink
if off, sir. (Aimwell *drinks*.) And how d'ye find yourself now, sir?

AIMWELL.

Somewhat better, though very faint still.   195

LADY BOUNTIFUL.

Ay, ay, people are always faint after these fits. —Come,
girls, you shall show the gentleman the house. —'Tis but
an old family building, sir, but you had better walk
about and cool by degrees than venture immediately
into the air. You'll find some tolerable pictures. 200
—Dorinda, show the gentleman the way. I must go to
the poor woman below.   *Exit.*

DORINDA.

This way, sir.

AIMWELL.

Ladies, shall I beg leave for my servant to wait on you,
for he understands pictures very well?   205

MRS. SULLEN.

Sir, we understand originals as well as he does pictures,
so he may come along.

Exeunt Dorinda, Mrs. Sullen, Aimwell, Archer, [Gipsy]. Aimwell
leads Dorinda.

Enter Foigard *and* Scrub, *meeting.*

FOIGARD.

Save you, Master Scrub.

SCRUB.

Sir, I won't be saved your way. I hate a priest, I abhor
the French, and I defy the devil. Sir, I'm a bold Briton 210
and will spill the last drop of my blood to keep out
popery and slavery.

FOIGARD.

Master Scrub, you would put me down in politics, and so
I would be speaking with Mrs. Shipsy.

---

206. *originals*] eccentric or singular persons; Mrs. Sullen also makes a
reference to original paintings.

SCRUB.

    Good Mr. Priest, you can't speak with her. She's sick, sir. 215
She's gone abroad, sir. She's—dead two months ago, sir.

                Enter Gipsy.

GIPSY.

    How now, impudence; how dare you talk so saucily to
the doctor? Pray, sir, don't take it ill, for the common
people of England are not so civil to strangers as—

SCRUB.

    You lie, you lie. 'Tis the common people that are civillest 220
to strangers.

GIPSY.

    Sirrah, I have a good mind to—get you out, I say.

SCRUB.

    I won't.

GIPSY.

    You won't, sauce-box? —Pray, doctor, what is the cap-
tain's name that came to your inn last night?   225

SCRUB.

    The captain! Ah, the devil, there she hampers me again.
The captain has me on one side, and the priest on
t'other. So between the gown and the sword I have a fine
time on't. But, *cedunt arma togae.*   *Going.*

GIPSY.

    What, sirrah, won't you march?   230

SCRUB.

    No, my dear, I won't march, but I'll walk. —[*Aside.*] And
I'll make bold to listen a little too.

            Goes behind the side-scene, and listens.

GIPSY.

    Indeed, doctor, the count has been barbarously treated,
that's the truth on't.

FOIGARD.

    Ah, Mrs. Gipsy, upon my shoul, now, gra, his complain- 235

---

   229. *cedunt arma togae*] Arms yield to the gown (Cf. Cicero *De Officiis*
1.22).

   235. *gra*] my dear; an exclamation ascribed to Irishmen. Also an exple-
tive expressing excitement or emotion. *OED* cites this scene, line 255
(below). The word was often written "arrah."

ings would mollify the marrow in your bones and move
the bowels of your commiseration. He veeps, and he
dances, and he fistles, and he swears, and he laughs, and
he stamps, and he sings. In conclusion, joy, he's afflicted
à la Francaise, and a stranger would not know whider to   240
cry or to laugh with him.

GIPSY.

What would you have me do, doctor?

FOIGARD.

Noting, joy, but only hide the count in Mrs. Sullen's
closet when it is dark.

GIPSY.

Nothing! Is that nothing? It would be both a sin and a   245
shame, doctor.

FOIGARD.

Here is twenty louis d'ors, joy, for your shame, and I will
give you an absolution for the shin.

GIPSY.

But won't that money look like a bribe?

FOIGARD.

Dat is according as you shall tauk it. If you receive the   250
money beforehand 'twill be *logicè* a bribe, but if you stay
till afterwards 'twill be only a gratification.

GIPSY.

Well, doctor, I'll take it *logicè*. But what must I do with
my conscience, sir?

FOIGARD.

Leave dat wid me, joy. I am your priest, gra, and your   255
conscience is under my hands.

GIPSY.

But should I put the count into the closet—

FOIGARD.

Vel, is dere any shin for a man's being in a closhet? One
may go to prayers in a closhet.

---

247. *louis d'ors*] a French gold coin first issued in the reign of Louis XIII
and subsequently until the time of Louis XVI.
251. *logicè*] in logic; according to logic.
252. *gratification*] a gratuity or reward.

GIPSY.

But if the lady should come into her chamber and go to 260
bed?

FOIGARD.

Vel, and is dere any shin in going to bed, joy?

GIPSY.

Ay, but if the parties should meet, doctor?

FOIGARD.

Vel den, the parties must be responsable. Do you be
after putting the count in the closet, and leave the shins 265
wid themselves. I will come with the count to instruct
you in your chamber.

GIPSY.

Well, doctor, your religion is so pure. Methinks I'm so
easy after an absolution and can sin afresh with so much
security that I'm resolved to die a martyr to't. Here's the 270
key of the garden-door. Come in the back way when 'tis
late. I'll be ready to receive you, but don't so much as
whisper. Only take hold of my hand; I'll lead you, and
do you lead the count and follow me.   *Exeunt.*

Enter Scrub.

SCRUB.

What witchcraft now have these two imps of the devil 275
been a-hatching here? There's twenty louis d'ors; I
heard that and saw the purse. But I must give room to
my betters.   *[Exit.]*

Enter Aimwell *leading* Dorinda, *and making love in dumb show;* Mrs.
Sullen *and* Archer.

MRS. SULLEN (*to* Archer).

Pray, sir, how d'ye like that piece?

ARCHER.

O, 'tis Leda. You find, madam, how Jupiter comes dis- 280
guised to make love.

MRS. SULLEN.

But what think you there of Alexander's battles?

---

280. *Leda*] the wife of Tyndareus, King of Sparta, seduced by Zeus in
the form of a swan.
282. *Alexander*] Alexander the Great, King of Macedon (356–323 B.C.).

ARCHER.

  We want only a Le Brun, madam, to draw greater battles
  and a greater general of our own. The Danube, madam,
  would make a greater figure in a picture than the   285
  Granicus, and we have our Ramillies to match their
  Arbela.

MRS. SULLEN.

  Pray, sir, what head is that in the corner there?

ARCHER.

  O, madam, 'tis poor Ovid in his exile.

MRS. SULLEN.

  What was he banished for?   290

ARCHER.

  His ambitious love, madam. (*Bowing.*)   His misfortune
  touches me.

MRS. SULLEN.

  Was he successful in his amours?

ARCHER.

  There he has left us in the dark. He was too much a
  gentleman to tell.   295

MRS. SULLEN.

  If he were secret I pity him.

ARCHER.

  And if he were successful I envy him.

MRS. SULLEN.

  How d'ye like that Venus over the chimney?

---

283. *Le Brun*] Charles Le Brun (1619–1690), first painter to Louis XIV
of France, noted for his series of pictures of Alexander's battles.

284–87. *a greater general . . . Arbela*] The greater general is, of course,
Marlborough, who defeated the French at Blenheim, in the Danube val-
ley, on 13 August 1704, and again at Ramillies, a Belgian village, on 23
May 1706. Alexander won his first great victory over the Persians at the
Granicus River in 334 B.C., and in 331 B.C. he defeated the armies of
Darius III at Arbela, an Assyrian town. It is ironic that *Alexander Crossing
the Granicus* is one of Le Brun's paintings for which Louis XIV posed as
Alexander.

289. *Ovid in his exile*] Publius Ovidius Naso (43 B.C.–A.D. 18), the Roman
poet, was banished to Tomi, on the western shore of the Black Sea, in A.D.
8, probably for his poem *Ars Amatoria* and for some offense against the
emperor. His name was connected with that of Augustus's daughter, the
dissolute Julia.

ARCHER.

Venus! I protest, madam, I took it for your picture, but
now I look again 'tis not handsome enough.   300

MRS. SULLEN.

Oh, what a charm is flattery! If you would see my picture, there it is over that cabinet. How d'ye like it?

ARCHER.

I must admire anything, madam, that has the least re-
semblance of you. But, methinks, madam—

He looks at the picture and Mrs. Sullen *three or four times, by turns.*

Pray, madam, who drew it?   305

MRS. SULLEN.

A famous hand, sir.   *Here* Aimwell *and* Dorinda *go off.*

ARCHER.

A famous hand, madam! Your eyes, indeed, are fea-
tured there, but where's the sparkling moisture, shining
fluid, in which they swim? The picture indeed has your
dimples, but where's the swarm of killing Cupids that 310
should ambush there? The lips too are figured out, but
where's the carnation dew, the pouting ripeness that
tempts the taste in the original?

MRS. SULLEN [*aside*].

Had it been my lot to have matched with such a man!

ARCHER.

Your breasts too. Presumptuous man! What, paint 315
heaven! Apropos, madam, in the very next picture is
Salmoneus, that was struck dead with lightning for offering to imitate Jove's thunder. I hope you served the
painter so, madam?

MRS. SULLEN.

Had my eyes the power of thunder they should employ 320
their lightning better.

ARCHER.

There's the finest bed in that room, madam. I suppose
'tis your ladyship's bedchamber.

---

317. *Salmoneus*] a son of Aeolus who imitated Zeus's thunder by driving
about in a bronze chariot. For this impiety Zeus destroyed him with a
thunderbolt.

MRS. SULLEN.

And what then, sir?

ARCHER.

I think that the quilt is the richest that ever I saw. I can't 325
at this distance, madam, distinguish the figures of the
embroidery. Will you give me leave, madam—

MRS. SULLEN [aside].

The devil take his impudence. Sure if I gave him an
opportunity he durst not offer it. I have a great mind to
try.   *Going.* 330

Returns.

S'death, what am I doing? And alone too! —Sister, sister?   *Runs out.*

ARCHER.

I'll follow her close,
     For where a Frenchman durst attempt to storm,
     A Briton sure may well the work perform. *Going.* 335

Enter Scrub.

SCRUB.

Martin, Brother Martin.

ARCHER.

O, Brother Scrub, I beg your pardon, I was not a-going.
Here's a guinea my master ordered you.

SCRUB.

A guinea, hi, hi, hi, a guinea! Eh, by this light it is a
guinea, but I suppose you expect one and twenty shil- 340
lings in change.

ARCHER.

Not at all; I have another for Gipsy.

SCRUB.

A guinea for her! Faggot and fire for the witch! Sir, give
me that guinea, and I'll discover a plot.

ARCHER.

A plot!   345

SCRUB.

Ay, sir, a plot, and a horrid plot. First, it must be a plot
because there's a woman in't. Secondly, it must be a
plot because there's a priest in't. Thirdly, it must be
a plot because there's French gold in't. And fourthly, it

must be a plot because I don't know what to make on't. 350

ARCHER.

Nor anybody else, I'm afraid, Brother Scrub.

SCRUB.

Truly I'm afraid so too, for where there's a priest and a woman there's always a mystery and a riddle. This I know, that here has been the doctor with a temptation in one hand and an absolution in the other, and Gipsy has 355 sold herself to the devil. I saw the price paid down; my eyes shall take their oath on't.

ARCHER.

And is all this bustle about Gipsy?

SCRUB.

That's not all. I could hear but a word here and there, but I remember they mentioned a count, a closet, a back 360 door, and a key.

ARCHER.

The count! Did you hear nothing of Mrs. Sullen?

SCRUB.

I did hear some word that sounded that way, but whether it was Sullen or Dorinda I could not distinguish. 365

ARCHER.

You have told this matter to nobody, brother?

SCRUB.

Told! No, sir, I thank you for that. I'm resolved never to speak one word pro nor con till we have a peace.

ARCHER.

You're i'th'right, Brother Scrub. Here's a treaty a-foot between the count and the lady. The priest and the 370 chambermaid are the plenipotentiaries. It shall go hard but I find a way to be included in the treaty. Where's the doctor now?

SCRUB.

He and Gipsy are this moment devouring my lady's marmalade in the closet. 375

AIMWELL (*from without*).

Martin, Martin.

ARCHER.

I come, sir, I come.

SCRUB.

But you forget the other guinea, Brother Martin.

ARCHER.

Here, I give it with all my heart.

SCRUB.

And I take it with all my soul.   [*Exit* Archer.] 380
Icod, I'll spoil your plotting, Mrs. Gipsy, and if you
should set the captain upon me these two guineas will
buy me off.   *Exit.*

Enter Mrs. Sullen *and* Dorinda *meeting.*

MRS. SULLEN.

Well, sister.

DORINDA.

And well, sister.   385

MRS. SULLEN.

What's become of my lord?

DORINDA.

What's become of his servant?

MRS. SULLEN.

Servant! He's a prettier fellow and a finer gentleman by
fifty degrees than his master.

DORINDA.

O' my conscience, I fancy you could beg that fellow at 390
the gallows-foot.

MRS. SULLEN.

O' my conscience, I could, provided I could put a friend
of yours in his room.

DORINDA.

You desired me, sister, to leave you when you transgres-
sed the bounds of honor.   395

MRS. SULLEN.

Thou dear censorious country girl. What dost mean?

380. S.D. *Exit* Archer] *Inchbald;*
Exeunt severally Q1.

390–91. *you ... gallows-foot*] Occasionally a condemned criminal's life
was spared when a respectable woman agreed to marry him. To beg a
person was to petition the Court of Wards for his or her custody. Mrs.
Sullen uses the term somewhat loosely.

You can't think of the man without the bedfellow, I find.

DORINDA.

I don't find anything unnatural in that thought; while
the mind is conversant with flesh and blood it must
conform to the humors of the company.   400

MRS. SULLEN.

How a little love and good company improves a woman.
Why, child, you begin to live. You never spoke before.

DORINDA.

Because I was never spoke to. My lord has told me that I
have more wit and beauty than any of my sex, and truly
I begin to think the man is sincere.   405

MRS. SULLEN.

You're in the right, Dorinda. Pride is the life of a woman, and flattery is our daily bread. And she's a fool that
won't believe a man there as much as she that believes
him in anything else. But I'll lay you a guinea that I had
finer things said to me than you had.   410

DORINDA.

Done. What did your fellow say to ye?

MRS. SULLEN.

My fellow took the picture of Venus for mine.

DORINDA.

But my lover took me for Venus herself.

MRS. SULLEN.

Common cant! Had my spark called me a Venus directly
I should have believed him a footman in good earnest. 415

DORINDA.

But my lover was upon his knees to me.

MRS. SULLEN.

And mine was upon his tiptoes to me.

DORINDA.

Mine vowed to die for me.

MRS. SULLEN.

Mine swore to die with me.

DORINDA.

Mine spoke the softest moving things.   420

---

419. *die*] achieve sexual climax.

MRS. SULLEN.

Mine had his moving things too.

DORINDA.

Mine kissed my hand ten thousand times.

MRS. SULLEN.

Mine has all that pleasure to come.

DORINDA.

Mine offered marriage.

MRS. SULLEN.

O Lard! D'ye call that a moving thing?   425

DORINDA.

The sharpest arrow in his quiver, my dear sister. Why,
my ten thousand pounds may lie brooding here this
seven years and hatch nothing at last but some ill-natured
clown like yours. Whereas, if I marry my Lord Aimwell
there will be title, place, and precedence, the park, 430
the play, and the drawing-room, splendor, equipage,
noise, and flambeaux. —"Hey, my Lady Aimwell's servants there—Lights, lights to the stairs—My Lady Aimwell's coach put forward—Stand by; make room for her
Ladyship."—Are not these things moving? What, 435
melancholy of a sudden?

MRS. SULLEN.

Happy, happy sister! Your angel has been watchful for
your happiness whilst mine has slept regardless of his
charge. Long smiling years of circling joys for you but
not one hour for me!   *Weeps.* 440

DORINDA.

Come, my dear, we'll talk of something else.

MRS. SULLEN.

O, Dorinda, I own myself a woman, full of my sex, a
gentle, generous soul, easy and yielding to soft desires, a
spacious heart where love and all his train might lodge.
And must the fair apartment of my breast be made a 445
stable for a brute to lie in?

DORINDA.

Meaning your husband, I suppose.

---

432. *flambeaux*] torches.

MRS. SULLEN.

Husband! No. Even husband is too soft a name for him.
But, come, I expect my brother here tonight or tomor-
row. He was abroad when my father married me.   450
Perhaps he'll find a way to make me easy.

DORINDA.

Will you promise not to make yourself easy in the meantime with my lord's friend?

MRS. SULLEN.

You mistake me, sister. It happens with us, as among the
men, the greatest talkers are the greatest cowards; and   455
there's a reason for it: those spirits evaporate in prattle
which might do more mischief if they took another
course. Though to confess the truth, I do love that fellow. And if I met him dressed as he should be, and I
undressed as I should be—look ye, sister, I have no   460
supernatural gifts. I can't swear I could resist the temptation, though I can safely promise to avoid it; and that's as
much as the best of us can do.

Exeunt Mrs. Sullen *and* Dorinda.

[IV.ii]   *Scene changes to the inn.*
                Enter Aimwell *and* Archer *laughing.*

ARCHER.

And the awkward kindness of the good motherly old
gentlewoman—

AIMWELL.

And the coming easiness of the young one. S'death, 'tis
pity to deceive her.

ARCHER.

Nay, if you adhere to those principles stop where you   5
are.

AIMWELL.

I can't stop, for I love her to distraction.

ARCHER.

S'death, if you love her a hair's breadth beyond discretion you must go no farther.

0.1 *Scene changes to the inn*] O; om.
Q1.

AIMWELL.

Well, well, anything to deliver us from sauntering away   10
our idle evenings at White's, Tom's, or Will's, and be
stinted to bear looking at our old acquaintance, the
cards, because our impotent pockets can't afford us a
guinea for the mercenary drabs.

ARCHER.

Or be obliged to some purse-proud coxcomb for a scan-   15
dalous bottle, where we must not pretend to our share
of the discourse because we can't pay our club o'th'reckoning. Damn it, I had rather sponge upon Morris and
sup upon a dish of bohea scored behind the door.

AIMWELL.

And there expose our want of sense by talking criticisms   20
as we should our want of money by railing at the government.

ARCHER.

Or be obliged to sneak into the side-box and between
both houses steal two acts of a play, and because we han't
money to see the other three we come away discon-   25
tented and damn the whole five.

AIMWELL.

And ten thousand such rascally tricks, had we outlived
our fortunes among our acquaintance. But now—

ARCHER.

Ay, now is the time to prevent all this. Strike while the
iron is hot. This priest is the luckiest part of our adven-   30

---

11. *Tom's*] This coffeehouse, called after Captain Thomas West, was at
No. 17 Russell Street. Like Will's, it seems to have been patronized by a
literary clientele.

17–18. *club o'th'reckoning*] share of the bill.

18. *Morris*] most likely the owner of Morris's coffeehouse, located in
Essex Street, the Strand, between 1702 and 1714.

19. *bohea*] at the beginning of the eighteenth century, the finest kind of
black tea.

19. *scored . . . door*] Records of customers' accounts were kept by means of
marks made by chalk on doors, walls, or slates. Originally, these marks
were incised on tallies.

23–24. *between . . . play*] Payment for boxes was not collected until after
the second act, until which time one could leave without paying. The two
major theaters at this time were the Queen's Theatre in the Haymarket,
where *The Beaux' Stratagem* was first performed, and Drury Lane Theatre.

ture. He shall marry you and pimp for me.

AIMWELL.

But I should not like a woman that can be so fond of a
Frenchman.

ARCHER.

Alas, sir, necessity has no law. The lady may be in dis-
tress. Perhaps she has a confounded husband, and her   35
revenge may carry her farther than her love. Igad, I
have so good an opinion of her, and of myself, that
I begin to fancy strange things; and we must say this for
the honor of our women, and indeed of ourselves, that
they do stick to their men as they do to their Magna   40
Charta. If the plot lies as I suspect I must put on the
gentleman. But here comes the doctor. I shall be ready. *Exit.*

Enter Foigard.

FOIGARD.

Sauve you, noble friend.

AIMWELL.

O, sir, your servant. Pray, doctor, may I crave your
name?   45

FOIGARD.

Fat naam is upon me? My naam is Foigard, joy.

AIMWELL.

Foigard, a very good name for a clergyman. Pray, Doctor Foigard, were you ever in Ireland?

FOIGARD.

Ireland! No, joy. Fat sort of plaace is dat saam Ireland?
Dey say de people are catcht dere when dey are young.   50

AIMWELL.

And some of 'em when they're old, as for example—
(*Takes* Foigard *by the shoulder.*)   Sir, I arrest you as a
traitor against the government. You're a subject of England and this morning showed me a commission by
which you served as chaplain in the French army. This is   55
death by our law, and your reverence must hang for't.

FOIGARD.

Upon my shoul, noble friend, dis is strange news you tell

---

47. *Foigard ... clergyman*] The name literally means "keeper of the
faith."

me—Fader Foigard a subject of England, de son of a
burgomaster of Brussels, a subject of England!
Ubooboo—   60

AIMWELL.

The son of a bogtrotter in Ireland. Sir, your tongue
will condemn you before any bench in the kingdom.

FOIGARD.

And is my tongue all your evidensh, joy?

AIMWELL.

That's enough.

FOIGARD.

No, no, joy, for I vill never spake English no more.   65

AIMWELL.

Sir, I have other evidence. —Here, Martin, you know
this fellow.

Enter Archer.

ARCHER (*in a brogue*).

Saave you, my dear cussen, how does your health?

FOIGARD (*aside*).

Ah, upon my shoul, dere is my countryman, and his
brogue will hang mine. —*Mynheer, Ick wet neat watt hey*   70
zacht; Ick universton ewe neat, sacramant.

AIMWELL.

Altering your language won't do, sir. This fellow knows
your person and will swear to your face.

FOIGARD.

Faace, fey, is dere a brogue upon my faash, too?

ARCHER.

Upon my soulvation, dere ish, joy. But Cussen Mack-   75
shane, vil you not put a remembrance upon me?

FOIGARD (*aside*).

Mackshane! By St. Paatrick, dat is naame, shure enough.

74. dere] *W2;* dear *Q1.*

---

60. *Ubooboo*] supposedly a typical Irish interjection. It seems to resemble
words meaning "fie," "nonsense," or "O, strange."
   61. *bogtrotter*] a nickname for Irishmen.
   70–71. *Mynheer . . . sacramant*] rather peculiar "Flemish" for "Sir, I don't
know what he is saying; I don't understand you, I swear."

AIMWELL.
    I fancy, Archer, you have it.

FOIGARD.
    The devil hang you, joy. By fat acquaintance are you my
    cussen?   80

ARCHER.
    O, de devil hang yourshelf, joy. You know we were little
    boys togeder upon de school, and your foster moder's
    son was married upon my nurse's chister, joy, and so we
    are Irish cussens.

FOIGARD.
    De devil taak the relation! Vel, joy, and fat school was it?   85

ARCHER.
    I tinks is vas—aay—'twas Tipperary.

FOIGARD.
    No, no, joy, it vas Kilkenny.

AIMWELL.
    That's enough for us—self-confession. Come, sir, we
    must deliver you into the hands of the next magistrate.

ARCHER.
    He sends you to jail, you're tried next assizes, and away   90
    you go swing into purgatory.

FOIGARD.
    And is it so wid you, cussen?

ARCHER.
    It vil be sho wid you, cussen, if you don't immediately
    confess the secret between you and Mrs. Gipsy. Look'ee,
    sir, the gallows or the secret; take your choice.   95

FOIGARD.
    The gallows! Upon my shoul, I hate that saam gallow,
    for it is a diseash dat is fatal to our family. —Vel den,
    dere is nothing, shentlemens, but Mrs. Shullen would
    spaak wid the count in her chamber at midnight, and
    dere is no haarm, joy, for I am to conduct the count to   100
    the plash myshelf.

ARCHER.
    As I guessed. Have you communicated the matter to the
    count?

---

90. *assizes*] circuit courts held periodically in each county.

FOIGARD.

I have not sheen him since.

ARCHER.

Right again. Why then, doctor, you shall conduct me to 105
the lady instead of the count.

FOIGARD.

Fat, my cussen to the lady! Upon my shoul, gra, dat is
too much upon the brogue.

ARCHER.

Come, come, doctor, consider we have got a rope about
your neck, and if you offer to squeak we'll stop your 110
windpipe most certainly. We shall have another job for
you in a day or two, I hope.

AIMWELL.

Here's company coming this way. Let's into my chamber
and there concert our affair farther.

ARCHER.

Come, my dear cussen, come along. *Exeunt.* 115

Enter Boniface, Hounslow *and* Bagshot *at one door,* Gibbet *at the opposite.*

GIBBET.

Well, gentlemen, 'tis a fine night for our enterprise.

HOUNSLOW.

Dark as hell.

BAGSHOT.

And blows like the devil. Our landlord here has showed
us the window where we must break in and tells us the
plate stands in the wainscot cupboard in the parlor. 120

BONIFACE.

Ay, ay, Mr. Bagshot, as the saying is, knives and forks
and cups and cans and tumblers and tankards. There's
one tankard, as the saying is, that's near upon as big as
me. It was a present to the squire from his godmother
and smells of nutmeg and toast like an East India ship. 125

---

125. *smells . . . ship*] Toast was frequently soaked in water, wine, or other
beverage, to which was sometimes added nutmeg and sugar. Richard
Steele (*Tatler* 24) states that rural justices of the peace often fed on this
toast before undertaking their duties. It is likely that it was also a popular

HOUNSLOW.

Then you say we must divide at the stairhead?

BONIFACE.

Yes, Mr. Hounslow, as the saying is. At one end of that
gallery lies my Lady Bountiful and her daughter and at
the other, Mrs. Sullen. As for the squire—

GIBBET.

He's safe enough. I have fairly entered him, and he's 130
more than half seas over already. But such a parcel of
scoundrels are got about him now that, Igad, I was
ashamed to be seen in their company.

BONIFACE.

'Tis now twelve, as the saying is. Gentlemen, you must
set out at one.   135

GIBBET.

Hounslow, do you and Bagshot see our arms fixed, and
I'll come to you presently.

HOUNSLOW. BAGSHOT.

We will.   *Exeunt.*

GIBBET.

Well, my dear Bonny, you assure me that Scrub is a
coward.   140

BONIFACE.

A chicken, as the saying is. You'll have no creature to
deal with but the ladies.

GIBBET.

And I can assure you, friend, there's a great deal of
address and good manners in robbing a lady. I am the
most a gentleman that way that ever traveled the road. 145
But, my dear Bonny, this prize will be a galleon, a Vigo
business. I warrant you we shall bring off three or four
thousand pound.

BONIFACE.

In plate, jewels, and money, as the saying is, you may.

---

refreshment on ships bringing nutmeg and other spices from the East
Indian islands.

130. *entered him*] started him (drinking).

146. *Vigo*] In Sir George Rooke's defeat of the French and Spanish
navies at Vigo Bay on 12 October 1702, booty reputedly worth at least
£1,000,000 fell into the hands of the victors.

GIBBET.

> Why then, Tyburn, I defy thee. I'll get up to town, sell   150
> off my horse and arms, buy myself some pretty em-
> ployment in the household, and be as snug and as hon-
> est as any courtier of 'um all.

BONIFACE.

> And what think you then of my daughter Cherry for a
> wife?   155

GIBBET.

> Look'ee, my dear Bonny, Cherry "is the goddess I
> adore," as the song goes, but it is a maxim that man and
> wife should never have it in their power to hang one
> another, for if they should the Lord have mercy on 'um
> both.   *Exeunt.* 160

End of the Fourth Act.

152. household] *Q1;* law *W2.*   153. any courtier] *Q1;* e'er a long
                                              gown *W2.*

---

150. *Tyburn*] the place in London where criminals were publicly executed.

152. *the household*] the royal household, the court.

156–57. *Cherry . . . goes*] At least as Gibbet quotes it, this song (about
Cherry or any other female) does not seem to be recorded in any of the
usual listings. Claude M. Simpson suggests to me that Gibbet might possibly allude to a version of a broadside, "The Yeoman's Delight, "beginning
"There is a Lass whom I adore" (Pepys Collection, 3,169, Cambridge).

ACT V

[V.i]   *Scene continues. Knocking without.*
                    Enter Boniface.

BONIFACE.
   Coming, coming. —A coach and six foaming horses at
   this time o'night! Some great man, as the saying is, for
   he scorns to travel with other people.

                    Enter Sir Charles Freeman.

SIR CHARLES.
   What, fellow, a public house, and a-bed when other
   people sleep?   5
BONIFACE.
   Sir, I an't a-bed, as the saying is.
SIR CHARLES.
   Is Mr. Sullen's family a-bed, think'ee?
BONIFACE.
   All but the squire himself, sir, as the saying is; he's in the
   house.
SIR CHARLES.
   What company has he?   10
BONIFACE.
   Why, sir, there's the constable, Mr. Gage the exiseman,
   the hunchbacked barber, and two or three other gen-
   tlemen.
SIR CHARLES.
   I find my sister's letters gave me the true picture of her
   spouse.   15

                    Enter Sullen *drunk.*

BONIFACE.
   Sir, here's the squire.
SULLEN.
   The puppies left me asleep. —Sir.
SIR CHARLES.
   Well, sir.

                            – 101 –

SULLEN.

Sir, I'm an unfortunate man. I have three thousand
pound a year, and I can't get a man to drink a cup of ale   20
with me.

SIR CHARLES.

That's very hard.

SULLEN.

Ay, sir, and unless you have pity upon me and smoke
one pipe with me, I must e'en go home to my wife, and I
had rather go to the devil by half.   25

SIR CHARLES.

But I presume, sir, you won't see your wife tonight.
She'll be gone to bed. You don't use to lie with your wife
in that pickle?

SULLEN.

What, not lie with my wife! Why, sir, do you take me for
an atheist or a rake?   30

SIR CHARLES.

If you hate her, sir, I think you had better lie from her.

SULLEN.

I think so too, friend, but I'm a justice of peace and must
do nothing against the law.

SIR CHARLES.

Law! As I take it, Mr. Justice, nobody observes law for
law's sake, only for the good of those for whom it was   35
made.

SULLEN.

But if the law orders me to send you to jail you must lie
there, my friend.

SIR CHARLES.

Not unless I commit a crime to deserve it.

SULLEN.

A crime! Oons, an't I married?   40

SIR CHARLES.

Nay, sir, if you call marriage a crime you must disown it
for a law.

SULLEN.

Eh! I must be acquainted with you, sir. But, sir, I should

25. go to] *Q2;* go *Q1.*   *spelling from 16th to 18th centuries)*
37. jail] gaol *W2;* goal *(a common*   *Q1.*

be very glad to know the truth of this matter.

SIR CHARLES.

Truth, sir, is a profound sea, and few there be that dare   45
wade deep enough to find out the bottom on't. Besides,
sir, I'm afraid the line of your understanding mayn't be
long enough.

SULLEN.

Look'ee, sir, I have nothing to say to your sea of truth,
but if a good parcel of land can intitle a man to a little   50
truth I have as much as any he in the country.

BONIFACE.

I never heard your worship, as the saying is, talk so
much before.

SULLEN.

Because I never met with a man that I liked before.

BONIFACE.

Pray, sir, as the saying is, let me ask you one question: 55
are not man and wife one flesh?

SIR CHARLES.

You and your wife, Mr. Guts, may be one flesh because
ye are nothing else, but rational creatures have minds
that must be united.

SULLEN.

Minds!   60

SIR CHARLES.

Ay, minds, sir. Don't you think that the mind takes place
of the body?

SULLEN.

In some people.

SIR CHARLES.

Then the interest of the master must be consulted be-

56–62. *are . . . body*] Larson points out a number of passages in the
divorce tracts (two of which follow) that suggest Milton's influence here:
"There is no true mariage between them, who agree not in true consent of
mind" — *Judgement of Martin Bucer (Prose Works*, 2:445); "Mariage is a
human society, and . . . all human society must proceed from the mind
rather than the body, els it would be but a kind of animal or beastish
meeting; if the mind therfore cannot have that due company by mariage,
that it may reasonably and humanly desire, that mariage can be no human
society, but a certain formalitie, or gilding over of little better then a
brutish congresse" (ibid., p. 275).

fore that of his servant.   65

SULLEN.

Sir, you shall dine with me tomorrow. Oons, I always
thought that we were naturally one.

SIR CHARLES.

Sir, I know that my two hands are naturally one because
they love one another, kiss one another, help one
another in all the actions of life, but I could not say so   70
much if they were always at cuffs.

SULLEN.

Then 'tis plain that we are two.

SIR CHARLES.

Why don't you part with her, sir?

SULLEN.

Will you take her, sir?

SIR CHARLES.

With all my heart.   75

SULLEN.

You shall have her tomorrow morning, and a venison
pasty into the bargain.

SIR CHARLES.

You'll let me have her fortune too?

SULLEN.

Fortune! Why, sir, I have no quarrel at her fortune. I
only hate the woman, sir, and none but the woman shall   80
go.

SIR CHARLES.

But her fortune, sir—

SULLEN.

Can you play at whisk, sir?

SIR CHARLES.

No, truly, sir.

SULLEN.

Nor at all fours?   85

---

71. *at cuffs*] fighting, at blows.

85. *all fours*] *OED*, which cites this passage, quotes Samuel Johnson: "a
low game at cards, played by two; so named from the four particulars by
which it is reckoned, and which, joined in the hand of either of the parties
are said to make *all fours*. The *all four* are *high, low, Jack,* and *the game.*"

SIR CHARLES.
   Neither!
SULLEN (*aside*).
   Oons, where was this man bred? —Burn me, sir, I can't
   go home; 'tis but two o'clock.
SIR CHARLES.
   For half an hour, sir, if you please. But you must con-
   sider 'tis late.   90
SULLEN.
   Late! That's the reason I can't go to bed. Come, sir.
                                                   Exeunt.

Enter Cherry, *runs across the stage and knocks at Aimwell's chamber
door. Enter* Aimwell *in his nightcap and gown.*

AIMWELL.
   What's the matter? You tremble, child; you're frighted.
CHERRY.
   No wonder, sir. But in short, sir, this very minute a gang
   of rogues are gone to rob my Lady Bountiful's house.
AIMWELL.
   How!   95
CHERRY.
   I dogged 'em to the very door and left 'em breaking in.
AIMWELL.
   Have you alarmed anybody else with the news?
CHERRY.
   No, no, sir, I wanted to have discovered the whole plot
   and twenty other things to your man Martin, but I have
   searched the whole house and can't find him. Where is   100
   he?
AIMWELL.
   No matter, child. Will you guide me immediately to the
   house?
CHERRY.
   With all my heart, sir. My Lady Bountiful is my god-
   mother, and I love Mrs. Dorinda so well.   105
AIMWELL.
   Dorinda! The name inspires me; the glory and the
   danger shall be all my own. —Come, my life, let me but
   get my sword.   *Exeunt.*

[V.ii] *Scene changes to a bedchamber in Lady Bountiful's house.*
Enter Mrs. Sullen, Dorinda *undressed; a table and lights.*

DORINDA.

'Tis very late, sister. No news of your spouse yet?

MRS. SULLEN.

No, I'm condemned to be alone till towards four, and
then perhaps I may be executed with his company.

DORINDA.

Well, my dear, I'll leave you to your rest. You'll go directly to bed, I suppose.   5

MRS. SULLEN.

I don't know what to do, hey-hoe.

DORINDA.

That's a desiring sigh, sister.

MRS. SULLEN.

This is a languishing hour, sister.

DORINDA.

And might prove a critical minute if the pretty fellow
were here.   10

MRS. SULLEN.

Here! What, in my bedchamber at two o'clock o'th'
morning, I undressed, the family asleep, my hated husband abroad, and my lovely fellow at my feet? O, gad,
sister!

DORINDA.

Thoughts are free, sister, and them I allow you. So, my   15
dear, good night.

MRS. SULLEN.

A good rest to my dear Dorinda.—   [*Exit* Dorinda.]
Thoughts free! Are they so? Why then suppose him
here, dressed like a youthful, gay, and burning bride-
groom,   20

Here Archer *steals out of the closet.*

with tongue enchanting, eyes bewitching, knees implor-
ing.

Turns a little o' one side, and sees Archer *in the posture she describes.*
Ah! (*Shrieks, and runs to the other side of the stage.*)   Have
my thoughts raised a spirit? —What are you, sir, a man
or a devil?   25

ARCHER.
A man, a man, madam.   *Rising.*

MRS. SULLEN.
How shall I be sure of it?

ARCHER.
Madam, I'll give you demonstration this minute.
                                           Takes her hand.

MRS. SULLEN.
What, sir, do you intend to be rude?

ARCHER.
Yes, madam, if you please.   30

MRS. SULLEN.
In the name of wonder, whence came ye?

ARCHER.
From the skies, madam. I'm a Jupiter in love, and you
shall be my Alcmena.

MRS. SULLEN.
How came you in?

ARCHER.
I flew in at the window, madam. Your cousin Cupid lent   35
me his wings, and your sister Venus opened the case-
ment.

MRS. SULLEN.
I'm struck dumb with admiration.

ARCHER.
And I with wonder.   *Looks passionately at her.*

MRS. SULLEN.
What will become of me?   40

ARCHER.
How beautiful she looks. The teeming jolly spring smiles
in her blooming face, and when she was conceived her
mother smelt to roses, looked on lilies.
    Lilies unfold their white, their fragrant charms
    When the warm sun thus darts into their arms.   45
                                           Runs to her.

---

33. Alcmena] *Q2;* Alimena *Q1.*

---

33. *Alcmena*] the wife of Amphitryon; while her husband was away at
war, she was seduced by Jupiter disguised as Amphitryon.
43. *smelt to*] smelt at; a common locution up to the nineteenth century.

MRS. SULLEN (*shrieks*).

Ah!

ARCHER.

Oons, madam, what d'ye mean? You'll raise the house.

MRS. SULLEN.

Sir, I'll wake the dead before I bear this. What, approach me with the freedoms of a keeper! I'm glad on't. Your impudence has cured me.   50

ARCHER (*kneels*).

If this be impudence I leave to your partial self. No panting pilgrim after a tedious, painful voyage e'er bowed before his saint with more devotion.

MRS. SULLEN (*aside*).

Now, now, I'm ruined if he kneels! —[*To him.*] Rise, thou prostrate engineer. Not all thy undermining skill   55 shall reach my heart. Rise, and know I am a woman without my sex. I can love to all the tenderness of wishes, sighs, and tears, but go no farther. Still to convince you that I'm more than woman, I can speak my frailty, confess my weakness even for you, but—   60

ARCHER.

For me!   *Going to lay hold on her.*

MRS. SULLEN.

Hold, sir, build not upon that. For my most mortal hatred follows if you disobey what I command you. Now! Leave me this minute. —(*Aside.*) If he denies, I'm lost.   65

ARCHER.

Then you'll promise—

MRS. SULLEN.

Anything another time.

ARCHER.

When shall I come?

MRS. SULLEN.

Tomorrow when you will.

---

55. *engineer*] plotter. Among other duties, military engineers were responsible for undermining enemy fortifications.

57. *without my sex*] "beyond the capacity or comprehension of" my sex (*OED*).

ARCHER.

Your lips must seal the promise.   70

MRS. SULLEN.

Pshaw!

ARCHER.

They must, they must. (*Kisses her.*)   Raptures and
paradise! And why not now, my angel? The time, the
place, silence, and secrecy all conspire; and the now conscious stars have preordained this moment for my hap-   75
piness.   *Takes her in his arms.*

MRS. SULLEN.

You will not, cannot, sure.

ARCHER.

If the sun rides fast and disappoints not mortals of tomorrow's dawn, this night shall crown my joys.

MRS. SULLEN.

My sex's pride assist me.   80

ARCHER.

My sex's strength help me.

MRS. SULLEN.

You shall kill me first.

ARCHER.

I'll die with you.   *Carrying her off.*

MRS. SULLEN.

Thieves, thieves, murther!

Enter Scrub *in his breeches and one shoe.*

SCRUB.

Thieves, thieves, murther, popery!   85

ARCHER.

Ha, the very timorous stag will kill in rutting time.

Draws and offers to stab Scrub.

SCRUB (*kneeling*).

O, pray, sir, spare all I have and take my life.

MRS. SULLEN (*holding Archer's hand*).

What does the fellow mean?

76. S.D. *in his arms*] C; *in her arms*
Q1.

SCRUB.

> O, madam, down upon your knees, your marrowbones.
> He's one of 'um.   90

ARCHER.

> Of whom?

SCRUB.

> One of the rogues—I beg your pardon, sir—one of the
> honest gentlemen that just now are broke into the
> house.

ARCHER.

> How!   95

MRS. SULLEN.

> I hope you did not come to rob me?

ARCHER.

> Indeed I did, madam, but I would have taken nothing
> but what you might ha' spared; but your crying thieves
> has waked this dreaming fool, and so he takes 'em for
> granted.   100

SCRUB.

> Granted! 'Tis granted, sir. Take all we have.

MRS. SULLEN.

> The fellow looks as if he were broke out of Bedlam.

SCRUB.

> Oons, madam, they're broke into the house with fire
> and sword; I saw them, heard them. They'll be here this
> minute.   105

ARCHER.

> What, thieves?

SCRUB.

> Under favor, sir, I think so.

MRS. SULLEN.

> What shall we do, sir?

ARCHER.

> Madam, I wish your ladyship a good night.

MRS. SULLEN.

> Will you leave me?   110

ARCHER.

> Leave you! Lord, madam, did you not command me to

---

102. *Bedlam*] the Hospital of St. Mary of Bethlehem, an asylum for the
insane.

be gone just now upon pain of your immortal hatred?

MRS. SULLEN.

Nay, but pray, sir—   *Takes hold of him.*

ARCHER.

Ha, ha, ha, now comes my turn to be ravished. You see
now, madam, you must use men one way or other. But 115
take this by the way, good madam, that none but a fool
will give you the benefit of his courage unless you'll take
his love along with it. —How are they armed, friend?

SCRUB.

With sword and pistol, sir.

ARCHER.

Hush, I see a dark lanthorn coming through the gallery. 120
Madam, be assured I will protect you or lose my life.

MRS. SULLEN.

Your life! No, sir, they can rob me of nothing that I
value half so much. Therefore now, sir, let me intreat
you to be gone.

ARCHER.

No, madam, I'll consult my own safety for the sake of 125
yours. I'll work by stratagem. Have you courage enough
to stand the appearance of 'em?

MRS. SULLEN.

Yes, yes. Since I have 'scaped your hands I can face
anything.

ARCHER.

Come hither, Brother Scrub, don't you know me?   130

SCRUB.

Eh, my dear brother, let me kiss thee.   *Kisses* Archer.

ARCHER.

This way—here—

Archer *and* Scrub *hide behind the bed. Enter* Gibbet *with a dark lanthorn in one hand and a pistol in t'other.*

GIBBET.

Ay, ay, this is the chamber, and the lady alone.

MRS. SULLEN.

Who are you, sir? What would you have? D'ye come to
rob me?   135

GIBBET.

Rob you! Alack a day, madam, I'm only a younger
brother, madam, and so, madam, if you make a noise I'll
shoot you through the head. But don't be afraid,
madam. (*Laying his lanthorn and pistol upon the table.*)
These rings, madam; don't be concerned, madam; I   140
have a profound respect for you, madam; your keys,
madam; don't be frighted, madam; I'm the most of a
gentleman. (*Searching her pockets.*)   This necklace,
madam; I never was rude to a lady; I have a veneration
—for this necklace—   145

Here Archer *having come round and seized the pistol, takes* Gibbet *by
the collar, trips up his heels, and claps the pistol to his breast.*

ARCHER.

Hold, profane villain, and take the reward of thy sac-
rilege.

GIBBET.

Oh, pray, sir, don't kill me; I an't prepared.

ARCHER.

How many is there of 'em, Scrub?

SCRUB.

Five and forty, sir.   150

ARCHER.

Then I must kill the villain to have him out of the way.

GIBBET.

Hold, hold, sir, we are but three, upon my honor.

ARCHER.

Scrub, will you undertake to secure him?

SCRUB.

Not I, sir. Kill him, kill him!

ARCHER.

Run to Gipsy's chamber; there you'll find the doctor.   155
Bring him hither presently.   *Exit* Scrub *running.*
Come, rogue, if you have a short prayer, say it.

GIBBET.

Sir, I have no prayer at all. The government has pro-

139. S.D. *pistol*] O; *pistols* Q1.

136–37. *only . . . brother*] Under the laws of primogeniture only eldest
sons inherited, making it necessary for their younger brothers to provide
for themselves.

vided a chaplain to say prayers for us on these occasions.

MRS. SULLEN.

Pray, sir, don't kill him. You fright me as much as him.   160

ARCHER.

The dog shall die, madam, for being the occasion of my
disappointment. —Sirrah, this moment is your last.

GIBBET.

Sir, I'll give you two hundred pound to spare my life.

ARCHER.

Have you no more, rascal?

GIBBET.

Yes, sir, I can command four hundred, but I must re-   165
serve two of 'em to save my life at the sessions.

Enter Scrub *and* Foigard.

ARCHER.

Here, doctor, I suppose Scrub and you between you
may manage him. Lay hold of him, doctor.

                                    Foigard *lays hold of* Gibbet.

GIBBET.

What, turned over to the priest already? —Look ye, doctor, you come before your time; I an't condemned yet,   170
I thank ye.

FOIGARD.

Come, my dear joy, I vill secure your body and your
shoul too. I vill make you a good Catholic and give you
an absolution.

GIBBET.

Absolution! Can you procure me a pardon, doctor?   175

FOIGARD.

No, joy.

GIBBET.

Then you and your absolution may go to the devil.

ARCHER.

Convey him into the cellar; there bind him. Take the
pistol, and if he offers to resist shoot him through the
head. And come back to us with all the speed you can.   180

---

166. *sessions*] the periodical sittings of justices of the peace or other
magistrates.

SCRUB.

Ay, ay, come, doctor. Do you hold him fast, and I'll
guard him.

> [*Exeunt* Foigard *and* Scrub *with* Gibbet.]

MRS. SULLEN.

But how came the doctor?

ARCHER.

In short, madam— (*Shrieking without.*) S'death, the
rogues are at work with the other ladies. I'm vexed I 185
parted with the pistol, but I must fly to their assistance.
—Will you stay here, madam, or venture yourself with
me?

MRS. SULLEN.

O, with you, dear sir, with you.

> *Takes him by the arm and exeunt.*

[V.iii] *Scene changes to another apartment in the same house.*
Enter Hounslow *dragging in* Lady Bountiful, *and* Bagshot *hauling
in* Dorinda; *the rogues with swords drawn.*

HOUNSLOW.

Come, come, your jewels, mistress.

BAGSHOT.

Your keys, your keys, old gentlewoman.

> *Enter* Aimwell *and* Cherry.

AIMWELL.

Turn this way, villains. I durst engage an army in such a
cause.   *He engages 'em both.*

DORINDA.

O, madam, had I but a sword to help the brave man!   5

LADY BOUNTIFUL.

There's three or four hanging up in the hall, but they
won't draw. I'll go fetch one, however.   *Exit.*

> *Enter* Archer *and* Mrs. Sullen.

ARCHER.

Hold, hold, my lord; every man his bird, pray.

---

8. *every man his bird*] Archer means that each of them should pick out his
own man to fight. The phrase was undoubtedly used by those shooting at
game birds.

They engage man to man; the rogues are thrown and disarmed.

CHERRY.

What, the rogues taken! Then they'll impeach my
father. I must give him timely notice.   *Runs out.*   10

ARCHER.

Shall we kill the rogues?

AIMWELL.

No, no, we'll bind them.

ARCHER.

Ay, ay. —(*To* Mrs. Sullen, *who stands by him.*)   Here,
madam, lend me your garter.

MRS. SULLEN [*aside*].

The devil's in this fellow. He fights, loves, and banters,   15
all in a breath. —Here's a cord that the rogues brought
with 'em, I suppose.

ARCHER.

Right, right, the rogue's destiny, a rope to hang himself.
—Come, my lord. This is but a scandalous sort of an
office (*binding the rogues together*) if our adventures   20
should end in this sort of hangman-work, but I hope
there is something in prospect that—

Enter Scrub.

Well, Scrub, have you secured your tartar?

SCRUB.

Yes, sir, I left the priest and him disputing about religion.   25

AIMWELL.

And pray carry these gentlemen to reap the benefit of
the controversy.

Delivers the prisoners to Scrub, *who leads 'em out.*

MRS. SULLEN.

Pray, sister, how came my lord here?

DORINDA.

And pray, how came the gentleman here?

MRS. SULLEN.

I'll tell you the greatest piece of villainy—   30

They talk in dumb show.

---

23. *tartar*] a rough or violent person.

AIMWELL.

I fancy, Archer, you have been more successful in your
adventures than the housebreakers.

ARCHER.

No matter for my adventure; yours is the principal.
Press her this minute to marry you, now while she's
hurried between the palpitation of her fear and the joy   35
of her deliverance, now while the tide of her spirits are
at high flood. Throw yourself at her feet, speak some
romantic nonsense or other, address her like Alexander
in the height of his victory, confound her senses, bear
down her reason, and away with her. The priest is now   40
in the cellar and dare not refuse to do the work.

Enter Lady Bountiful.

AIMWELL.

But how shall I get off without being observed?

ARCHER.

You a lover and not find a way to get off! —Let me see—

AIMWELL.

You bleed, Archer.

ARCHER.

S'death, I'm glad on't. This wound will do the business.   45
I'll amuse the old lady and Mrs. Sullen about dressing
my wound while you carry off Dorinda.

LADY BOUNTIFUL.

Gentlemen, could we understand how you would be
gratified for the services—

ARCHER.

Come, come, my lady, this is no time for compliments.   50
I'm wounded, madam.

LADY BOUNTIFUL. MRS. SULLEN.

How! Wounded!

DORINDA.

I hope, sir, you have received no hurt?

AIMWELL.

None but what you may cure.   *Makes love in dumb show.*

LADY BOUNTIFUL.

Let me see your arm, sir. —I must have some powder   55
sugar to stop the blood. —O me, an ugly gash! Upon my
word, sir, you must go into bed.

ARCHER.

Ay, my lady, a bed would do very well. —(*To* Mrs. Sullen.) Madam, will you do me the favor to conduct me to a chamber?   60

LADY BOUNTIFUL.

Do, do, daughter, while I get the lint and the probe and the plaster ready.

Runs out one way; Aimwell *carries off* Dorinda *another.*

ARCHER.

Come, madam, why don't you obey your mother's commands?

MRS. SULLEN.

How can you, after what is past, have the confidence to   65
ask me?

ARCHER.

And if you go to that, how can you, after what is past, have the confidence to deny me? Was not this blood shed in your defense and my life exposed for your protection? Look ye, madam, I'm none of your romantic   70
fools that fight giants and monsters for nothing. My valor is downright Swiss. I'm a soldier of fortune and must be paid.

MRS. SULLEN.

'Tis ungenerous in you, sir, to upbraid me with your services.   75

ARCHER.

'Tis ungenerous in you, madam, not to reward 'em.

MRS. SULLEN.

How, at the expense of my honor?

ARCHER.

Honor! Can honor consist with ingratitude? If you would deal like a woman of honor, do like a man of honor. D'ye think I would deny you in such a case?   80

Enter a Servant.

SERVANT.

Madam, my lady ordered me to tell you that your brother is below at the gate.   [*Exit* Servant.]

---

72. *Swiss*] mercenary. French monarchs hired Swiss soldiers for their bodyguards. The Vatican still employs Swiss guards.

MRS. SULLEN.

My brother? Heavens be praised. —Sir, he shall thank
you for your services; he has it in his power.

ARCHER.

Who is your brother, madam?   85

MRS. SULLEN.

Sir Charles Freeman. You'll excuse me, sir, I must go
and receive him.   [Exit.]

ARCHER.

Sir Charles Freeman! S'death and hell! My old acquaintance. Now unless Aimwell had made good use of his
time, all our fair machine goes souse into the sea like the   90
Eddystone.   Exit.

[V.iv]   Scene changes to the gallery in the same house.
              Enter Aimwell and Dorinda.

DORINDA.

Well, well, my lord, you have conquered. Your late
generous action will, I hope, plead for my easy yielding,
though I must own your lordship had a friend in the
fort before.

AIMWELL.

The sweets of Hybla dwell upon her tongue. —Here,   5
doctor—

              Enter Foigard with a book.

FOIGARD.

Are you prepared boat?

DORINDA.

I'm ready. —But first, my lord, one word. I have a
frightful example of a hasty marriage in my own family.

---

91. *Eddystone*] The first Eddystone lighthouse, built by Henry Winstanley off the coast of Cornwall between 1696 and 1699, was destroyed by a
storm on 27 November 1703. Winstanley, who was in the lighthouse at the
time, drowned.
[V.iv]
5. *Hybla*] Hybla Minor (also Megara Hyblea), in ancient times a city on
the east coast of Sicily about twelve miles north of Syracuse. It is thought
that the celebrated Hyblean honey, often mentioned by the poets, was
produced in the area. The city has often been confused with Hybla on
Mount Etna (Hybla Major).

When I reflect upon't, it shocks me. Pray, my lord, con-   10
sider a little.

AIMWELL.

Consider! Do you doubt my honor or my love?

DORINDA.

Neither. I do believe you equally just as brave. And were
your whole sex drawn out for me to choose, I should not
cast a look upon the multitude if you were absent. But,   15
my lord, I'm a woman. Colors, concealments may hide a
thousand faults in me; therefore know me better first. I
hardly dare affirm I know myself in anything except my
love.

AIMWELL (aside).

Such goodness who could injure? I find myself unequal   20
to the task of villain; she has gained my soul and made it
honest like her own. I cannot, cannot hurt her. —[To
Foigard.] Doctor, retire.   Exit Foigard.
Madam, behold your lover and your proselyte, and
judge of my passion by my conversion. I'm all a lie, nor   25
dare I give a fiction to your arms. I'm all counterfeit
except my passion.

DORINDA.

Forbid it, heaven! A counterfeit!

AIMWELL.

I am no lord, but a poor needy man come with a mean, a
scandalous design to prey upon your fortune. But the   30
beauties of your mind and person have so won me from
myself that like a trusty servant I prefer the interest of
my mistress to my own.

DORINDA.

Sure I have had the dream of some poor mariner, a
sleepy image of a welcome port, and wake involved in   35
storms. —Pray, sir, who are you?

AIMWELL.

Brother to the man whose title I usurped but stranger to
his honor or his fortune.

DORINDA.

Matchless honesty! Once I was proud, sir, of your wealth

24. *proselyte*] a convert.

and title but now am prouder that you want it. Now I 40
can show my love was justly leveled and had no aim but
love. —Doctor, come in.

Enter Foigard *at one door,* Gipsy *at another, who whispers* Dorinda.

Your pardon, sir, we shan't want you now. —[*To* Aim-
well.] Sir, you must excuse me. I'll wait on you pre-
sently.   *Exit with* Gipsy. 45
FOIGARD.
Upon my shoul now, dis is foolish.   *Exit.*
AIMWELL.
Gone, and bid the priest depart! It has an ominous look.

Enter Archer.

ARCHER.
Courage, Tom. Shall I wish you joy?
AIMWELL.
No.
ARCHER.
Oons, man, what ha' you been doing?   50
AIMWELL.
O, Archer, my honesty I fear has ruined me.
ARCHER.
How!
AIMWELL.
I have discovered myself.
ARCHER.
Discovered! And without my consent? What, have I em-
barked my small remains in the same bottom with yours, 55
and you dispose of all without my partnership?
AIMWELL.
O, Archer, I own my fault.
ARCHER.
After conviction—'tis then too late for pardon. You may
remember, Mr. Aimwell, that you proposed this folly.
As you begun, so end it. Henceforth I'll hunt my for- 60
tune single. So farewell.

43–44. we shan't want you now   now, sir? *Q2;* We sha'not, won't you
. . . Sir,] *D2;* we shannot; won't you   now, sir? *C,W2;* we shan't want you
now, sir? *Q1;* we shall not want you   now, sir. *W6.*

55. *bottom*] a ship.

AIMWELL.

Stay, my dear Archer, but a minute.

ARCHER.

Stay! What, to be despised, exposed, and laughed at?
No, I would sooner change conditions with the worst of
the rogues we just now bound than bear one scornful   65
smile from the proud knight that once I treated as my
equal.

AIMWELL.

What knight?

ARCHER.

Sir Charles Freeman, brother to the lady that I had
almost—but no matter for that; 'tis a cursed night's   70
work, and so I leave you to make your best on't.   *Going.*

AIMWELL.

Freeman! —One word, Archer. Still I have hopes.
Methought she received my confession with pleasure.

ARCHER.

S'death! Who doubts it?

AIMWELL.

She consented after to the match, and still I dare believe   75
she will be just.

ARCHER.

To herself, I warrant her, as you should have been.

AIMWELL.

By all my hopes, she comes, and smiling comes.

Enter Dorinda *mighty gay.*

DORINDA.

Come, my dear lord, I fly with impatience to your arms.
The minutes of my absence was a tedious year. Where's   80
this tedious priest?

Enter Foigard.

ARCHER.

Oons, a brave girl.

DORINDA.

I suppose, my lord, this gentleman is privy to our affairs?

ARCHER.

Yes, yes, madam. I'm to be your father.   85

DORINDA.

Come, priest, do your office.

ARCHER.

Make haste, make haste, couple 'em any way. (*Takes Aimwell's hand.*) Come, madam, I'm to give you—

DORINDA.

My mind's altered. I won't.

ARCHER.

Eh—   90

AIMWELL.

I'm confounded.

FOIGARD.

Upon my shoul, and sho is myshelf.

ARCHER.

What's the matter now, madam?

DORINDA.

Look ye, sir, one generous action deserves another. This gentleman's honor obliged him to hide nothing from   95
me; my justice engages me to conceal nothing from him.
In short, sir, you are the person that you thought you
counterfeited. You are the true Lord Viscount Aimwell,
and I wish your lordship joy. Now, priest, you may be
gone. If my lord is pleased now with the match let his   100
lordship marry me in the face of the world.

AIMWELL. ARCHER.

What does she mean?

DORINDA.

Here's a witness for my truth.

Enter Sir Charles *and* Mrs. Sullen.

SIR CHARLES.

My dear Lord Aimwell, I wish you joy.

AIMWELL.

Of what?   105

SIR CHARLES.

Of your honor and estate. Your brother died the day
before I left London, and all your friends have writ after
you to Brussels; among the rest I did myself the honor.

ARCHER.

Hark ye, Sir Knight, don't you banter now?

SIR CHARLES.

'Tis truth, upon my honor.   110

AIMWELL.

Thanks to the pregnant stars that formed this accident.

ARCHER.

Thanks to the womb of time that brought it forth. Away
with it.

AIMWELL.

Thanks to my guardian angel that led me to the prize.

Taking Dorinda's hand.

ARCHER.

And double thanks to the noble Sir Charles Freeman. 115
—My lord, I wish you joy. —My lady, I wish you joy. —I-
gad, Sir Freeman, you're the honestest fellow living.
—S'death, I'm grown strange airy upon this matter.—
My lord, how d'ye? A word, my lord, how d'ye? A word,
my lord: don't you remember something of a previous 120
agreement that entitles me to the moiety of this lady's
fortune, which I think will amount to five thousand
pound?

AIMWELL.

Not a penny, Archer. You would ha' cut my throat just
now because I would not deceive this lady.   125

ARCHER.

Ay, and I'll cut your throat again if you should deceive
her now.

AIMWELL.

That's what I expected, and to end the dispute the lady's
fortune is ten thousand pound. We'll divide stakes. Take
the ten thousand pound or the lady.   130

DORINDA.

How! Is your lordship so indifferent?

---

118. *airy*] lively, merry, vivacious.

ARCHER.

No, no, no, madam, his lordship knows very well that I'll take the money. I leave you to his lordship, and so we're both provided for.

Enter Count Bellair.

COUNT.

Mesdames et Messieurs, I am your servant trice humble. I   135
hear you be rob here.

AIMWELL.

The ladies have been in some danger, sir.

COUNT.

And begar, our inn be rob too.

AIMWELL.

Our inn! By whom?

COUNT.

By the landlord, begar. Garzoon, he has rob himself and   140
run away.

ARCHER.

Robbed himself!

COUNT.

Ay, begar, and me too of a hundre pound.

ARCHER.

A hundred pound.

COUNT.

Yes, that I owed him.   145

AIMWELL.

Our money's gone, Frank.

ARCHER.

Rot the money! My wench is gone. *Savez vous quelque chose de Mademoiselle Cherry?*

Enter a Fellow *with a strongbox and a letter.*

FELLOW.

Is there one Martin here?

134.1–145. *Enter* Count Bellair . . .   *lines substituted in W6.*
I owed him] *Q1; see Appendix A for*

147–48. *Savez vous . . . Cherry*] Do you know anything about Miss Cherry?

ARCHER.

    Ay, ay, who wants him?   150

FELLOW.

    I have a box here and letter for him.

ARCHER (*taking the box*).

    Ha, ha, ha, what's here? Legerdemain! By this light, my
lord, our money again. But this unfolds the riddle.
(*Opening the letter, reads.*)   Hum, hum, hum. O, 'tis for
the public good and must be communicated to the com-   155
pany.

    "Mr. Martin,

    My father being afraid of an impeachment by the
rogues that are taken tonight is gone off, but if you
can procure him a pardon he will make great discov-   160
eries that may be useful to the country. Could I have
met you instead of your master tonight I would have
delivered myself into your hands with a sum that
much exceeds that in your strongbox, which I have
sent you, with an assurance to my dear Martin that I   165
shall ever be his most faithful friend till death.

                              CHERRY BONIFACE."

There's a billet-doux for you. As for the father, I think
he ought to be encouraged, and for the daughter, pray,
my lord, persuade your bride to take her into her service   170
instead of Gipsy.

AIMWELL.

    I can assure you, madam, your deliverance was owing
to her discovery.

DORINDA.

    Your command, my lord, will do without the obligation.
I'll take care of her.   175

SIR CHARLES.

    This good company meets opportunely in favor of a
design I have in behalf of my unfortunate sister. I intend to part her from her husband. Gentlemen, will you
assist me?

ARCHER.

    Assist you! S'death, who would not?   180

---

152. *Legerdemain*] sleight of hand, trickery, deception.
168. *billet-doux*] love letter.

COUNT.

Assist! Garzoon, we all assist.

Enter Sullen.

SULLEN.

What's all this? They tell me, spouse, that you had like to have been robbed.

MRS. SULLEN.

Truly, spouse, I was pretty near it, had not these two gentlemen interposed.   185

SULLEN.

How came these gentlemen here?

MRS. SULLEN.

That's his way of returning thanks, you must know.

COUNT.

Garzoon, the question be apropos for all dat.

SIR CHARLES.

You promised last night, sir, that you would deliver your lady to me this morning.   190

SULLEN.

Humph.

ARCHER.

Humph. What do you mean by humph? Sir, you shall deliver her. In short, sir, we have saved you and your family, and if you are not civil we'll unbind the rogues, join with 'um, and set fire to your house. —What does 195 the man mean? Not part with his wife!

COUNT.

Ay, garzoon, de man no understan common justice.

MRS. SULLEN.

Hold, gentlemen, all things here must move by consent; compulsion would spoil us. Let my dear and I talk the matter over, and you shall judge it between us.   200

SULLEN.

Let me know first who are to be our judges. —Pray, sir, who are you?

181–275. Assist . . . Then I will]   *in W6.*
Q1; see Appendix A for lines substituted   181. assist] *W2;* assest *Q1.*

SIR CHARLES.

I am Sir Charles Freeman, come to take away your wife.

SULLEN.

And you, good sir?

AIMWELL.

Thomas, Viscount Aimwell, come to take away your sis- 205
ter.

SULLEN.

And you, pray, sir?

ARCHER.

Francis Archer, Esquire, come—

SULLEN.

To take away my mother, I hope. —Gentlemen, you're
heartily welcome. I never met with three more obliging 210
people since I was born. —And now, my dear, if you
please, you shall have the first word.

ARCHER.

And the last, for five pound.

MRS. SULLEN.

Spouse.

SULLEN.

Rib.   215

MRS. SULLEN.

How long have we been married?

SULLEN.

By the almanac fourteen months, but by my account
fourteen years.

MRS. SULLEN.

'Tis thereabout by my reckoning.

COUNT.

Garzoon, their account will agree.   220

MRS. SULLEN.

Pray, spouse, what did you marry for?

SULLEN.

To get an heir to my estate.

SIR CHARLES.

And have you succeeded?

205. Thomas] *Inchbald;* Charles *Q1.*

---

215. *Rib*] wife, woman; alluding to the creation of Eve from Adam's rib.

SULLEN.

No.

ARCHER.

The condition fails of his side. —Pray, madam, what did   225
you marry for?

MRS. SULLEN.

To support the weakness of my sex by the strength of
his and to enjoy the pleasures of an agreeable society.

SIR CHARLES.

Are your expectations answered?

MRS. SULLEN.

No.   230

COUNT.

A clear case, a clear case.

SIR CHARLES.

What are the bars to your mutual contentment?

MRS. SULLEN.

In the first place I can't drink ale with him.

SULLEN.

Nor can I drink tea with her.

MRS. SULLEN.

I can't hunt with you.   235

SULLEN.

Nor can I dance with you.

MRS. SULLEN.

I hate cocking and racing.

SULLEN.

And I abhor ombre and piquet.

MRS. SULLEN.

Your silence is intolerable.

SULLEN.

Your prating is worse.   240

MRS. SULLEN.

Have we not been a perpetual offense to each other, a
gnawing vulture at the heart?

---

237. *cocking*] cockfighting.
238. *ombre*] "a card-game played by three persons, with forty cards, the
eights, nines, and tens of the ordinary pack being thrown out" (*OED*).
238. *piquet*] "a card-game played by two persons with a pack of 32 cards
(the low cards from the two to the six being excluded)" (*OED*).

SULLEN.
A frightful goblin to the sight.
MRS. SULLEN.
A porcupine to the feeling.
SULLEN.
Perpetual wormwood to the taste.   245
MRS. SULLEN.
Is there on earth a thing we could agree in?
SULLEN.
Yes—to part.
MRS. SULLEN.
With all my heart.
SULLEN.
Your hand.
MRS. SULLEN.
Here.   250
SULLEN.
These hands joined us; these shall part us—away—
MRS. SULLEN.
North.
SULLEN.
South.
MRS. SULLEN.
East.
SULLEN.
West—far as the poles asunder.   255
COUNT.
Begar, the ceremony be vera pretty.
SIR CHARLES.
Now, Mr. Sullen, there wants only my sister's fortune to
make us easy.
SULLEN.
Sir Charles, you love your sister, and I love her fortune;
every one to his fancy.   260
ARCHER.
Then you won't refund?
SULLEN.
Not a stiver.

---

245. *wormwood*] a plant noted for its bitter taste; consequently, anything
bitter or grievous.
262. *stiver*] a small coin of the Low Countries, of very little value.

ARCHER.

> Then I find, madam, you must e'en go to your prison again.

COUNT.

> What is the portion?   265

SIR CHARLES.

> Ten thousand pound, sir.

COUNT.

> Garzoon, I'll pay it, and she shall go home wid me.

ARCHER.

> Ha, ha, ha, French all over. —Do you know, sir, what ten thousand pound English is?

COUNT.

> No, begar, not justement.   270

ARCHER.

> Why, sir, 'tis a hundred thousand livres.

COUNT.

> A hundre tousand livres! A garzoon, me canno' do't. Your beauties and their fortunes are both too much for me.

ARCHER.

> Then I will. This night's adventure has proved strangely   275
> lucky to us all, for Captain Gibbet in his walk had made
> bold, Mr. Sullen, with your study and escritoire and
> had taken out all the writings of your estate, all the
> articles of marriage with this lady, bills, bonds, leases,
> receipts to an infinite value. I took 'em from him, and I   280
> deliver them to Sir Charles.

> *Gives him a parcel of papers and parchments.*

SULLEN.

> How, my writings! My head aches consumedly. —Well,
> gentlemen, you shall have her fortune—but I can't talk.
> If you have a mind, Sir Charles, to be merry and cele-
> brate my sister's wedding and my divorce, you may com-   285

---

279. this] *O; his QI.*

---

270. *justement*] exactly.
271. *livres*] a denomination of French money; a livre was divided into twenty sous.
277. *escritoire*] a writing desk. *OED* cites this passage.

mand my house—but my head aches consumedly.
—Scrub, bring me a dram.

ARCHER (*to* Mrs. Sullen).

Madam, there's a country dance to the trifle that I sung
today. Your hand, and we'll lead it up.

Here a dance.

'Twould be hard to guess which of these parties is the   290
better pleased,. the couple joined or the couple parted:
the one rejoicing in hopes of an untasted happiness and
the other in their deliverance from an experienced mis-
ery.

    Both happy in their several states we find,   295
Those parted by consent and those conjoined.
Consent, if mutual, saves the lawyer's fee;
Consent is law enough to set you free.

FINIS.

290. *Q1–2 and most eds. include S. P.*
ARCHER; *om. Gosse.*

295–98. *Both . . . free*] According to Larson (p. 176), "This was the great
idea of Milton's divorce tracts; the consent of both parties mutually given
is a cause fully sufficient for divorce." Milton maintains that if God has not
joined a couple, "then is there no power above their own consent to
hinder them from unjoyning"(*Prose Works,* 2:328) when their minds are
not "fitly dispos'd, and enabl'd to maintain a cherfull conversation, to the
solace and love of each other, according as God intended and promis'd in
the very first foundation of matrimony" (ibid.). Milton states further, in
Tetrachordon, that "there can be nothing in the equity of law, why divorce
by consent may not be lawfull" (ibid., p. 646).

AN EPILOGUE

Designed to be spoke in the *Beaux' Stratagem*

If to our play your judgment can't be kind,
Let its expiring author pity find;
Survey his mournful case with melting eyes,
Nor let the bard be damned before he dies.
Forbear you fair on his last scene to frown,   5
But his true exit with a plaudit crown;
Then shall the dying poet cease to fear
The dreadful knell while your applause he hears.
At Leuctra so, the conquering Theban died,
Claimed his friends' praises but their tears denied;   10
Pleased in the pangs of death he greatly thought
Conquest with loss of life but cheaply bought.
The difference this, the Greek was one would fight
As brave though not so gay as Sergeant Kite.
Ye sons of Will's, what's that to those who write?   15
To Thebes alone the Grecian owed his bays;
You may the bard above the hero raise,
Since yours is greater than Athenian praise.

---

2. *expiring author*] Although tradition has killed off Farquhar somewhat earlier, generally on one of his benefit nights, he must have died between 18 and 21 May 1707, for he was buried on 23 May. This reference suggests that Farquhar did not write the Epilogue. See Eric Rothstein, *George Farquhar* (New York, 1967), pp. 28-29.

9. *Leuctra . . . died*] Under the leadership of Epaminondas the Thebans defeated the Spartans at Leuctra in 371 B.C. Epaminondas did not die there, however, but nine years later at Mantinea, where the Spartans were defeated again.

14. *Kite*] the clever recruiting sergeant in Farquhar's *The Recruiting Officer* (1706).

15. *sons of Will's*] patrons of Will's Coffeehouse. See III.ii.91.

16. *bays*] the wreath of bay leaves awarded to a conqueror or a poet.

Appendix A

Variant Passages from *The Works,* Sixth Edition

[V.iv.134.1–145]

Enter Foigard.

FOIGARD.
    Arrah, fait, de people do say you be all robbed, joy.   135

AIMWELL.
    The ladies have been in some danger, sir, as you saw.

FOIGARD.
    Upon my shoul, our inn be rob too.

AIMWELL.
    Our inn! By whom?

FOIGARD.
    Upon my shalvation, our landlord has robbed himself
    and run away wid da money.   140

ARCHER.
    Robbed himself!

FOIGARD.
    Ay, fait, and me too of a hundre pound.

ARCHER.
    Robbed you of a hundred pound!

FOIGARD.
    Yes, fait, honey, that I did owe to him.

[Line 181]
    Ay, upon my shoul, we'll all asshist.

[Line 188]

FOIGARD.
    Ay, but upon my conshience, de question be apropos for
    all dat.

[Line 197]

FOIGARD.

Arrah, not part wid your wife! Upon my shoul, de man dosh not understand common shivility.

[Line 220]

FOIGARD.

Upon my conshience, dere accounts vil agree.

[Line 231]

FOIGARD.

Arrah, honey, a clear caase, a clear caase!

[Line 256]

FOIGARD.

Upon my shoul, a very pretty sheremony.

[Lines 265–66, 275; lines 267–74 from Q1 are not in W6]

ARCHER.

What is her portion?

SIR CHARLES.

Ten thousand pound, sir.

ARCHER.

I'll pay it. My lord, I thank him, has enabled me, and, if the lady pleases, she shall go home with me. This night's adventure . . . . (continue as in Q1).

Appendix B
Chronology

Approximate dates are indicated by *. Dates for plays are those on which they were first made public, either on stage on in print.

Political and Literary Events	Life and Major Works of Farquhar

1631
Death of Donne.
John Dryden born.

1633
Samuel Pepys born.

1635
Sir George Etherege born.*

1640
Aphra Behn born.

1641
William Wycherley born.*

1642
First Civil War began (ended (1646).
Theaters closed by Parliament.
Thomas Shadwell born.*

1648
Second Civil War.
Nathaniel Lee born.*

1649
Execution of Charles I.

1650
Jeremy Collier born.

1651
Hobbes's *Leviathan* published.

1652
First Dutch War began (ended 1654).
Thomas Otway born.

1656

D'Avenant's *THE SIEGE OF RHODES* performed at Rutland House.

1657

John Dennis born.

1658

Death of Oliver Cromwell.

D'Avenant's *THE CRUELTY OF THE SPANIARDS IN PERU* performed at the cockpit.

1660

Restoration of Charles II.

Theatrical patents granted to Thomas Killigrew and Sir William D'Avenant, authorizing them to form, respectively, the King's and the Duke of York's Companies.

Pepys began his diary.

1661

Cowley's *THE CUTTER OF COLMAN STREET*.

D'Avenant's *THE SIEGE OF RHODES* (expanded to two parts).

1662

Charter granted to the Royal Society.

1663

Dryden's *THE WILD GALLANT*.

Tuke's *THE ADVENTURES OF FIVE HOURS*.

1664

Sir John Vanbrugh born.

Dryden's *THE RIVAL LADIES*.

Dryden and Howard's *THE INDIAN QUEEN*.

Etherege's *THE COMICAL REVENGE*.

1665

Second Dutch War began (ended 1667).

Great Plague.

Dryden's *THE INDIAN EM-PEROR.*

Orrery's *MUSTAPHA.*

1666

Fire of London.

Death of James Shirley.

1667

Jonathan Swift born.

Milton's *Paradise Lost* published.

Sprat's *The History of the Royal Society* published.

Dryden's *SECRET LOVE.*

1668

Death of D'Avenant.

Dryden made Poet Laureate.

Dryden's *An Essay of Dramatic Poesy* published.

Shadwell's *THE SULLEN LOVERS.*

Etherege's *SHE WOULD IF SHE COULD.*

1669

Pepys terminated his diary.

Susanna Centlivre born.

1670

William Congreve born.

Dryden's *THE CONQUEST OF GRANADA*, Part I.

1671

Dorset Garden Theatre (Duke's Company) opened.

Colley Cibber born.

Milton's *Paradise Regained* and *Samson Agonistes* published.

Dryden's *THE CONQUEST OF GRANADA*, Part II.

THE REHEARSAL, by the Duke of Buckingham and others.

Wycherley's *LOVE IN A WOOD.*

1672

Third Dutch War began (ended 1674).

Joseph Addison born.

Richard Steele born.

Dryden's *MARRIAGE A LA MODE.*

1674

New Drury Lane Theatre (King's
Company) opened.

Death of Milton.

Nicholas Rowe born.

Thomas Rymer's *Reflections on Aristotle's Treatise of Poesy* (translation of
Rapin) published.

1675

Dryden's *AURENG-ZEBE.*

Wycherley's *THE COUNTRY
WIFE.**

1676

Etherege's *THE MAN OF MODE.*

Otway's *DON CARLOS.*

Shadwell's *THE VIRTUOSO.*

Wycherley's *THE PLAIN DEALER.*

1677

Rymer's *Tragedies of the Last Age
Considered* published.

Behn's *THE ROVER.*

Dryden's *ALL FOR LOVE.*

Lee's *THE RIVAL QUEENS.*

George Farquhar born.*

1678

Popish Plot.

Bunyan's *Pilgrim's Progress* (Part I)
published.

1679

Exclusion Bill introduced.

Death of Thomas Hobbes.

Death of Roger Boyle, Earl of Orrery.

Charles Johnson born.

1680

Death of Samuel Butler.

Death of John Wilmot, Earl of
Rochester.

Dryden's *THE SPANISH FRIAR.*

Lee's *LUCIUS JUNIUS BRUTUS.*

Otway's *THE ORPHAN.*

1681

Charles II dissolved Parliament at
Oxford.

Dryden's *Absalom and Achitophel*
published.

Tate's adaptation of *KING LEAR*.

1682

The King's and the Duke of York's
Companies merged into the
United Company.

Dryden's *The Medal, MacFlecknoe,*
and *Religio Laici* published.

Otway's *VENICE PRESERVED.*

1683

Rye House Plot.

Death of Thomas Killigrew.

Crowne's *CITY POLITIQUES.*

1685

Death of Charles II; accession of
James II.

Revocation of the Edict of Nantes.

The Duke of Monmouth's Rebellion.

Death of Otway.

John Gay born.

Crowne's *SIR COURTLY NICE.*

Dryden's *ALBION AND AL-
BANIUS.*

1687

Death of the Duke of Buckingham.

Dryden's *The Hind and the Panther*
published.

Newton's *Principia* published.

1688

The Revolution.

Alexander Pope born.

Shadwell's *THE SQUIRE OF AL-
SATIA.*

1689

The War of the League of Augsburg began (ended 1697).

Toleration Act.

Death of Behn.
Shadwell made Poet Laureate.
Dryden's *DON SEBASTIAN.*
Shadwell's *BURY FAIR.*

1690
Battle of the Boyne.
Locke's *Two Treatises of Government*
and *An Essay Concerning Human
Understanding* published.

1691
Death of Etherege.*
Langbaine's *An Account of the En-
glish Dramatic Poets* published.

1692
Death of Lee.
Death of Shadwell.
Tate made Poet Laureate.

1693
George Lillo born.*
Rymer's *A Short View of Tragedy*
published.
Congreve's *THE OLD BACHELOR.*

1694
Death of Queen Mary.   Entered Trinity College, Dublin.
Southerne's *THE FATAL MAR-
RIAGE.*

1695
Group of actors led by Thomas
Betterton left Drury Lane and es-
tablished a new company at Lin-
coln's Inn Fields.
Congreve's *LOVE FOR LOVE.*
Southerne's *OROONOKO.*

1696
Cibber's *LOVE'S LAST SHIFT.*
Vanbrugh's *THE RELAPSE.*

1697
Treaty of Ryswick ended the War   Went to London.
of the League of Augsburg.
Charles Macklin born.
Congreve's *THE MOURNING
BRIDE.*

Vanbrugh's *THE PROVOKED WIFE*.

1698

Collier controversy started with the publication of *A Short View of the Immorality and Profaneness of the English Stage*.

1699

LOVE AND A BOTTLE produced at Drury Lane in mid-December. *The Adventures of Covent Garden* (anecdotal narrative) published December 15.

THE CONSTANT COUPLE, OR A TRIP TO THE JUBILEE produced at Drury Lane in late November.

1700

Death of Dryden.

Blackmore's *Satire Against Wit* published.

Congreve's *THE WAY OF THE WORLD*.

1701

Act of Settlement.

War of the Spanish Succession began (ended 1713).

Death of James II.

Rowe's *TAMERLANE*.

Steele's *THE FUNERAL*.

SIR HARRY WILDAIR produced at Drury Lane in April. *Love and Business* (collection of prose and verse) published.

1702

Death of William III; accession of Anne.

The Daily Courant began publication.

Cibber's *SHE WOULD AND SHE WOULD NOT*.

THE INCONSTANT (adapted from Fletcher's *THE WILD GOOSE CHASE*) produced at Drury Lane in early March. *THE TWIN RIVALS* opened at Drury Lane on December 14.

1703

Death of Samuel Pepys.

Rowe's *THE FAIR PENITENT*.

Married to Margaret Pemell.

1704

Capture of Gibraltar; Battle of Blenheim.

Defoe's *The Review* began publication (1704–1713).

Swift's *A Tale of a Tub* and *The Battle of the Books* published.

Commissioned Lieutenant of Grenadiers. *THE STAGE-COACH* (comic afterpiece) produced at Lincoln's Inn Fields in January.

Cibber's *THE CARELESS HUS-BAND.*

1705

Haymarket Theatre opened.
Steele's *THE TENDER HUSBAND.*

1706

Battle of Ramillies.

1707

Union of Scotland and England.
Henry Fielding born.

Sent on recruiting duty to Lichfield and then to Shrewsbury.

THE RECRUITING OFFICER opened at Drury Lane on April 8.

Died in a London garret 18–21 May.

THE BEAUX' STRATAGEM opened at the Haymarket on March 8.

Love's Catechism (largely a patchwork of passages from *THE BEAUX' STRATAGEM*) published.

Barcelona (poem) published.*

1708

Downes's *Roscius Anglicanus* published.

1709

Samuel Johnson born.
Rowe's edition of Shakespeare published.
The Tatler began publication (1709–1711).
Centlivre's *THE BUSY BODY.*

1711

Shaftesbury's *Characteristics* published.
The Spectator began publication (1711–1712).
Pope's *An Essay on Criticism* published.

1713

Treaty of Utrecht ended the War of the Spanish Succession.
Addision's *CATO.*

1714

Death of Anne; accession of George I.
Steele became Governor of Drury

Lane.

John Rich assumed management of Lincoln's Inn Fields.

Centlivre's *THE WONDER: A WOMAN KEEPS A SECRET.*

Rowe's *JANE SHORE.*

1715

Jacobite Rebellion.

Death of Tate.

Rowe made Poet Laureate.

Death of Wycherley.

1716

Addison's *THE DRUMMER.*

1717

David Garrick born.

Cibber's *THE NON-JUROR.*

Gay, Pope, and Arbuthnot's *THREE HOURS AFTER MAR-RIAGE.*

1718

Death of Rowe.

Centlivre's *A BOLD STOKE FOR A WIFE.*

1719

Death of Addison.

Defoe's *Robinson Crusoe* published.

Young's *BUSIRIS, KING OF EGYPT.*

1720

South Sea Bubble.

Samuel Foote born.

Steele suspended from the Governorship of Drury Lane (restored 1721).

Little Theatre in the Haymarket opened.

Steele's *The Theatre* (periodical) published.

Hughes's *THE SIEGE OF DAMASCUS.*

1721

Walpole became first Minister.

1722
Steele's *THE CONSCIOUS LOV-
ERS.*

1723
Death of Centlivre.
Death of D'Urfey.

1725
Pope's edition of Shakespeare published.

1726
Death of Jeremy Collier.
Death of Vanbrugh.
Law's *Unlawfulness of Stage Enter-
tainments* published.
Swift's *Gulliver's Travels* published.

1727
Death of George I; accession of
George II.
Death of Sir Isaac Newton.
Arthur Murphy born.

1728
Pope's *The Dunciad* (first version)
published.
Cibber's *THE PROVOKED HUS-
BAND* (expansion of Vanbrugh's
fragment *A JOURNEY TO LON-
DON*).
Gay's *THE BEGGAR'S OPERA.*

1729
Goodman's Fields Theatre opened.
Death of Congreve.
Death of Steele.
Edmund Burke born.

1730
Cibber made Poet Laureate.
Oliver Goldsmith born.
Thomson's *The Seasons* published.
Fielding's *THE AUTHOR'S
FARCE; TOM THUMB* (revised as
THE TRAGEDY OF TRAGEDIES,
1731).

1731

Death of Defoe.

Fielding's *THE GRUB-STREET OPERA.*

Lillo's *THE LONDON MERCHANT.*

1732

Covent Garden Theatre opened.

Death of Gay.

George Colman the elder born.

Fielding's *THE COVENT GARDEN TRAGEDY.*

Fielding's *THE MODERN HUSBAND.*

Charles Johnson's *CAELIA.*

1733

Pope's *An Essay on Man* (Epistles I-III) published (Epistle IV, 1734).

1734

Death of Dennis.

The Prompter began publication (1734–1736).

Theobald's edition of Shakespeare published.

Fielding's *DON QUIXOTE IN ENGLAND.*

1736

Fielding led the "Great Mogul's Company of Comedians" at the Little Theatre in the Haymarket (1736–1737).

Fielding's *PASQUIN.*

Lillo's *FATAL CURIOSITY.*

1737

The Stage Licensing Act.

Dodsley's *THE KING AND THE MILLER OF MANSFIELD.*

Fielding's *THE HISTORICAL REGISTER FOR 1736.*